A HISTORY OF
POLICE
FIREARMS UNITS

A HISTORY OF POLICE FIREARMS UNITS

STEPHEN WYNN

PEN & SWORD HISTORY

AN IMPRINT OF PEN & SWORD BOOKS LTD.
YORKSHIRE · PHILADELPHIA

First published in Great Britain in 2025 by
Pen & Sword History
An imprint of
Pen & Sword Books Ltd
Yorkshire - Philadelphia

Copyright © Stephen Wynn, 2025

ISBN 978 1 52677 848 2

The right of Stephen Wynn to be identified as the Author of this work has been asserted by him in accordance with the Copyright, Designs and Patents Act 1988.

A CIP catalogue record for this book is available from the British Library.

All rights reserved. No part of this book may be reproduced, transmitted, downloaded, decompiled or reverse engineered in any form or by any means, electronic or mechanical including photocopying, recording or by any information storage and retrieval system, without permission from the Publisher in writing.
NO AI TRAINING: Without in any way limiting the Author's and Publisher's exclusive rights under copyright, any use of this publication to "train" generative artificial intelligence (AI) technologies to generate text is expressly prohibited. The Author and Publisher reserve all rights to license uses of this work for generative AI training and development of machine learning language models.

Typeset in INDIA by IMPEC eSolutions
Printed and bound in England by CPI Group (UK) Ltd, Croydon, CR0 4YY

The Publisher's authorised representative in the EU for product safety is Authorised Rep Compliance Ltd., Ground Floor, 71 Lower Baggot Street, Dublin D02 P593, Ireland.
www.arccompliance.com

For a complete list of Pen & Sword titles please contact:

PEN & SWORD BOOKS LIMITED
George House, Units 12 & 13, Beevor Street, Off Pontefract Road,
Barnsley, S71 1HN, UK
E-mail: enquiries@pen-and-sword.co.uk
Website: www.pen-and-sword.co.uk

or

PEN AND SWORD BOOKS
1950 Lawrence Rd, Havertown, PA 19083, USA
E-mail: Uspen-and-sword@casematepublishers.com
Website: www.penandswordbooks.com

Introduction

This book looks at police firearms units throughout England, Scotland, Wales, and Northern Ireland, and also includes other police forces such as the British Transport Police, the Ministry of Defence Police and the Civil Nuclear Constabulary. It looks back to the police's history of its use of firearms in more modern times, as well as how the increase of that use has continued over time and why that need has occurred.

From the 1960s and up until the early 1980s, the relationship the police had with firearms was nowhere near as professional as it is today. Back then, the police had a much more reactive approach to firearms-related incidents. It was more a case of wait for an incident to occur and then decide if police officers needed firearms to be able to deal with it safely. Even then it was simply a case of 'potluck' as to which police officers were on duty at the time. Some of the officers might have never worked together in a firearms sense before, which meant that they had no idea how those they were working with would react under pressure.

Officers who were designated 'shots' would have received little in the way of tactical awareness input; nearly all their training would have focused on being good at shooting at targets on a firearms range. It was as if police and firearms were a partnership that was not really wanted by senior officers, but were seen as a necessary evil, nevertheless.

As previously stated, the police's approach towards firearms had become much more professional by the late 1980s. This came about partly because of cases where the police had shot innocent people, such as Stephen Waldorf, in 1983, and Cherry Groce, in 1985, and also from shooting incidents such as the Shepherd's Bush Murders of 1966, and the Hungerford Massacre of 1987, both of which are looked at in greater detail in this book.

The book also looks at the timings and reasoning behind why nearly all police forces throughout the UK had formed full-time firearms units by the end of the 1980s, and how during the early 1990s, most had also developed the idea of Armed Response Vehicles (ARVs).

Personal accounts from those who served as firearms officers/instructors in different forces are included, especially from the early years of police firearms, and the book is completed by a look at some of the more well-known and well-documented police-related firearms incidents, some of which have been more contentious than others. The final aspect of the book also takes into account how the police's use of firearms has evolved and developed during this time, whilst also looking at the long-term mental and emotional impact on officers' lives; those who find themselves in situations where they have felt the need to open fire on suspects they believed were about to place their own life, or that of another, in imminent danger.

Contents

Introduction vii

Chapter One	A Brief History of Police Use of Firearms	1
Chapter Two	The Selection Process to Become a Police Firearms Officer	11
Chapter Three	Shooting and Tactics	20
Chapter Four	Public Perception	31
Chapter Five	Authorised Firearms Officers – AFOs	37
Chapter Six	A Personal Insight into Life as a Police Firearms Officer	43
Chapter Seven	The Police Firearms Situation in Northern Ireland	50
Chapter Eight	Cheshire Constabulary - A Brief History of their Firearms Unit	53
Chapter Nine	Essex Police – A Brief History of Their Central Firearms Unit	57
Chapter Ten	Leicestershire Police – A Brief History of Their Firearms Unit	60
Chapter Eleven	West Midlands Police – A Brief History of Their Firearms Unit	64
Chapter Twelve	Avon & Somerset, Gloucestershire, and Wiltshire's Tri-Force Specialist Operations Unit	77
Chapter Thirteen	Aidrian 'Aide' Smart: Ex-Firearms Instructor, Essex Police	80

Chapter Fourteen	Armed Robbers and Robberies During the 1960s and 1970s	93
Chapter Fifteen	The Shepherd's Bush Murders, 1966	97
Chapter Sixteen	The Clydesdale Bank Robbery, 1969	102
Chapter Seventeen	The Ramsey Incident, 1979	107
Chapter Eighteen	The Shooting of Stephen Waldorf, 1983	116
Chapter Nineteen	The Shooting of PC Brian 'Bill' Bishop, 1984	122
Chapter Twenty	The Shooting of Cherry Groce, 1985	134
Chapter Twenty-One	The Hungerford Massacre, 1987	138
Chapter Twenty-Two	The Sudanese Hijacking, 1996	150
Chapter Twenty-Three	The Shooting of James Ashley, 1998	158
Chapter Twenty-Four	The Shooting of Azelle Rodney, 2005	162
Chapter Twenty-Five	The Shooting of Jean Charles de Menezes, 2005	171
Chapter Twenty-Six	The Shooting of Raoul Moat, 2010	179
Chapter Twenty-Seven	The Shooting of Anthony Grainger, 2012	185
Chapter Twenty-Eight	The Shooting of Jermaine Baker, 2015	189
Chapter Twenty-Nine	The Murder of PC Keith Palmer, 2017	195
Chapter Thirty	The Borough Market Attack, 2017	198
Chapter Thirty-One	The Shooting of Chris Kaba, 2022	201

Conclusion 205
Appendix A: Territorial Police Forces in the UK 208
Appendix B: Weapons Used by UK Police Forces (2025) 210
Author Biography 213
Index 215

CHAPTER ONE

A Brief History of Police Use of Firearms

Throughout England, Northern Ireland, Scotland and Wales, there are a total of forty-five of what are known as territorial police forces (see Appendix A), and three special police forces: the British Transport Police, the Civil Nuclear Constabulary and the Ministry of Defence Police. All forty-eight of these forces have a firearms capacity, although the British Transport Police have only had such a capability since May 2011.

As the Metropolitan Police service is the largest, in so far as the number of officers it has, and is the oldest on the UK mainland, it makes sense to use them as an example in overall terms and as a direct comparison of policing up and down the country so far as firearms are concerned.

London's Metropolitan Police was founded by Sir Robert Peel, who at the time was the Home Secretary, on 29 September 1829, as part of the Metropolitan Police Act 1829. Its role was to police the newly formed Metropolitan Police District, which had a radius of 7 miles from its centre in Charing Cross, and included parts of Kent, Middlesex and Surrey. It did not include the City of London, which had its own force.

Prior to the formation of an 'official' police force, such work had been undertaken by a combination of night watchmen, parish constables and what were affectionately known as the Bow Street Runners. Before this new Act, policing across the country had been covered by what was known as the Statute of Winchester, which was established on 8 October 1285, during the time of the Norman Conquest. After nearly 600 years, the nation was certainly in need of some change in how it was policed. Up until the Metropolitan Police Act of 1829, any major acts of public disorder had been dealt with, and put down, by the British Army. It was time for change.

Ten years after its launch, the Metropolitan Police Act was updated and amalgamated the remaining few vestiges of law enforcement throughout London into the Metropolitan Police. This saw the end of the Bow Street Runners, and the Thames River Police, which had been founded in 1800 to tackle the ever-increasing acts of thefts from cargo ships in London's docks along the River Thames.

Even though firearms were in their infancy and were not widely available, especially to members of the public, the major towns and cities throughout the country could be extremely dangerous places for the very well off in society, or for large businesses who relied on their imported goods having to pass through the busy, overcrowded and ever-increasing dock areas of London.

The idea of a proper, full-time professional police service began with the half-brothers Henry and John Fielding in the mid-1700s. In 1748, Henry Fielding became the chief magistrate at Bow Street Magistrates' Court, in the City of Westminster, and in 1751 he wrote and published a report entitled, *An Enquiry into the Causes of the Late Increase of Robbers and Related Writings*, which in essence was about the rise in crime, particularly in London. Two of the main reasons for this, Fielding said, were that people found it easier to make more money by committing crime than they could by going out to work, and the other was an ineffective policing system.

It was in 1749, a year after Henry Fielding took up his new position, that he formed what become known as the Bow Street Runners; what many consider to be London's first full-time professional police force. Small in number, there were only six of them to begin with, but they quickly became a professional and effective body of men. They remained in existence until 1839, when its personnel became part of the Metropolitan Police. The Bow Street Runners were not a patrolling force but instead served writs and arrested individuals on the authority of the Bow Street Magistrates' Court. These were violent times, and although the Bow Street Runners were men who were more than capable of looking after themselves, they were not armed. All they had to protect themselves with were their fists against 'footpads' (a thief who robbed pedestrians on foot) and highwaymen, who more often than not were armed.

Fortunately, after the death of Henry Fielding in 1754, the Bow Street Runners remained in place because the man who succeeded him as chief magistrate was his blind half-brother, John Fielding, who remained in post until his own death in 1780. John improved on what his brother Henry had started by bringing in a mounted section of Bow Street Runners in 1805, who were nicknamed the Robin Redbreasts because of their red-coloured waistcoats.

After the formation of the Metropolitan Police in 1829, the number of similar forces was quickly replicated around the country and by 1851 there were approximately 13,000 policemen throughout England and Wales, although there was still no legal requirement for local authorities to form their own police forces. It was only after the passing through Parliament of the County and Borough Police Act of 1856 that policing became a requirement in every local authority throughout England and Wales. This new requirement was assisted and made easier because the funding for these new police forces came from central government.

From about 1885 until the turn of the century, officers who were engaged on night duties in certain parts of London had the choice as to whether they wished to go out on patrol armed with a Webley revolver. By 1900 there were 243 individual constabularies throughout England and Wales that were policed by a total of 46,800 men.

Although violence towards police constables was almost commonplace in the late 1800s and early 1900s, shootings were extremely rare, mainly because it was extremely difficult to gain possession of a firearm.

One of the first detailed incidents that resulted in an unarmed police officer being shot dead took place at 10:45am on Saturday, 23 January 1909 in the Tottenham area of north London, when two Russian refugees attacked a man carrying money to pay the wages of the men working at the Schnurrmann rubber factory. Shots were fired, which drew the attention of police officers at the nearby Tottenham Police station. Police Constable Newman and his colleague, Constable Tyler, who were both unarmed, ran out into the street to see what all the commotion was about. As they made their way into Chestnut Road, they saw two men firing pistols at another man, Ralph John Jocelyn, who was laying on the ground outside of the factory. On seeing the policemen, the two men turned and ran, but after a short while they stopped, turned around, and fired several shots at the advancing police officers before running off again.

A motor vehicle belonging to the rubber factory came along, which Constable Newman climbed onto, with Constable Tyler running alongside. The chase continued into Devon Road and on into Midgley Road, with the robbers repeatedly turning to fire upon their pursuers, who understandably were keeping a safe distance. When he felt the robbers' revolvers were empty of bullets, Constable Newman instructed the driver of the vehicle to speed up and run the two men down. Almost immediately, however, the two men opened fire again. One of the shots struck Constable Newman on his right cheek, but thankfully it was only a superficial wound.

The chase continued with Newman joining Constable Tyler and another officer, Constable Bond. They finally cornered the two men in Dowsett Road and it was at this time that Constable Tyler was shot dead when a round struck him in the head. One of the two men forced his way into Oakhill Cottage at the bottom of Dowsett Road, where he was confronted by the angry occupant, Mrs Eliza Rolstone.

Constable Eagles from Woodford Green police station made his way to Mrs Rolstone's cottage on his bicycle. When he arrived there was a crowd outside, with one member carrying a double-barrelled shotgun. Constable Eagles borrowed the gun and without any hesitation, or knowing what he was up against, made his way into the cottage. He ended up in a yard where he found a ladder and placed it up to an upstairs window, and whilst looking into what turned out to be a rear bedroom, a man appeared and pointed a revolver at him, causing him to quickly climb back down the ladder. By now a Detective Dixon had arrived, and Eagles borrowed his revolver as it was less cumbersome than the shotgun. The pair then cautiously re-entered the property, making their way upstairs to a closed door at the top. After he had climbed about three steps, Constable Eagles noticed a shadow of somebody coming from under the door. He fired two shots right through it, before it gradually started to open. A man appeared in the doorway and pointed his pistol at Constable Eagles, who fired once again. The man appeared to throw his arms in the air before falling backwards onto a bed in the room. Eagles quickly made his way up the stairs and into the room, where he once again opened fire. The man was in possession of a Mauser pistol that still had two rounds left: one in the breech and the other in the magazine.

A Doctor Alcock, who was in the area visiting some of his patients, made his way to the scene, but by the time he had arrived the shot man, who was subsequently identified by the name of Jacob, was already dead. Doctor Alcock gave the cause of the man's death as being a bullet wound in the right temple, an inch in front of the right ear.

Another early incident involving the shooting of unarmed police officers occurred on the evening of 16 December 1910, when police were called to an address in Houndsditch, which was located right next to a rented property and a jeweller. The occupant told the police on their arrival that she believed she could hear a tunnel being dug under the property. One of the police officers, Constable Bentley, entered the rented building and was immediately shot; his wounds were fatal. Three more police officers, constables Strongman, Choat and Tucker, all of whom were unarmed, were also shot dead by the gang.

The murder of these four young police officers caused outrage throughout the country. On New Year's Day 1911, information was received by the police that two of the gang responsible were hiding at 100 Sidney Street, London. What was to follow became known as the Sidney Street Siege, when the then Home Secretary, Winston Churchill, personally attended the scene.

On this occasion the incident was dealt with by both armed police officers, several of whom carried double-barrelled shotguns, and a company of soldiers from the Scots Guards, who were stationed nearby. During the ensuing siege, the upper level of the house where the two suspects were hiding mysteriously caught fire, forcing them both downstairs.

When the local fire brigade arrived on the scene, Churchill refused permission for them to approach the building to put out the fire. Not long afterwards, the upper floors of the building collapsed into the ground floor, engulfing it in flames and killing the two men inside.

Incidents such as this were basically how policing and the subject of firearms remained, with weapons being available for use as and when they were required, and then usually only by men who had experience with them, such as those who had previously served in the British Army.

During the First World War, police officers could carry a side arm whilst working during the hours of darkness. Throughout the 1920s and 1930s there were no real major incidents that required police officers to be armed as part of their general police duties, and from July 1936, a Sergeant could issue firearms if he felt there was a specific reason to do so. Everything changed, however, with the arrival of the Second World War. On 1 June 1940, 3,500 Canadian-made bolt action .303 rifles were issued to the police, most of which had last been used during the First World War but nevertheless were dusted down and handed over to the police.

During the war there was a need to arm large numbers of police officers who were required to carry out 'sentry' type duties outside such buildings as Buckingham Palace and 10 Downing Street, or locations it was believed could be a possible target for enemy saboteurs. Plans were also in place to arm the entire police service in the case of a German invasion, so that the police could readily assist the armed forces in defending the nation. At the end of the war, rather than retrieving all the weapons, it was decided that the weapons dumps already in place should be added to with more up-to-date weapons just in case another war broke out.

Several incidents took place throughout the 1960s, 1970s and 1980s, where either police officers were shot dead or members of the public were shot dead by the police, which in some cases, were innocent people. More information on several of these incidents can be found elsewhere in this book and brings us up to the present day.

For those officers who do not carry firearms, they are instead provided with an ASP (Armament Systems and Procedures) baton, which is essentially an extendable metallic-based truncheon, or a solid plastic version. They are also provided with different makes of hand-held incapacitant sprays, which are designed to sting a person's eyes. As of 2003, Authorised Firearms Officers (AFOs) were also authorised to carry a TASER, which in essence is a high voltage electric shock. It has two electrodes that are fired at a person using compressed nitrogen and are designed to penetrate both clothing and skin. The electrical currents delivered cause involuntary muscle contractions and disrupt the usual functions of a person's nervous system, making it impossible to move by preventing the brain from sending messages to the body's muscles. This is potentially a potent weapon and has led to some fatalities.

Over time changes have naturally been made, with the only police force throughout the United Kingdom that now has all its officers permanently armed being in Northern Ireland, although by way of comparison, England's largest police force, the Metropolitan Police Service, has a number of firearms requirements just because of the policing area they cover.

Currently, the Metropolitan Police has the Specialist Firearms Command. As of December 2018, it became known as SCO19, but for purely internal systems within the Metropolitan Police, it is also referred to as MO19, or Met Ops 19, to show where the Command sits within the organisation.

SCO19 is split into four sections: Armed Response Vehicle (ARV), Trojan Proactive Unit (TPU), Tactical Support Teams (TST) and Counter Terrorist Specialist Firearms Officers (CTSFO).

ARV

These are double-crewed vehicles whose officers are currently equipped with personal issue Glock 17 pistols, a TASER model X26, two MP5 carbines, as well as two G36 rifles. These vehicles respond to all firearms incidents and provide support for their unarmed colleagues. They are also tasked with carrying out directed patrols in areas with high gun crime.

TPU

These units are tasked to patrol in areas that have high records of gun-related crime, gang-related issues, and incidents of serious violence that are not necessarily gun-related.

TST

The Metropolitan Police has had TSTs for the past twenty years. It is their job to provide both covert and overt proactive support to operations in each area where it is deemed that firearms support might be required. The standard of ability required to be a member of this unit sits between that of an ARV officer and that of a Specialist Firearms Officer.

CTSFO

A member of a CTSFO team is one of the most highly trained firearms officers serving within the Metropolitan Police. They are also capable of working alongside firearms officers from other police forces and can deal with any type of firearms operation up to and including hostage situations and terrorist scenarios.

The Metropolitan Police has several specialist firearms units. These include what is known as 'Protection Command', which is one of the commands within the forces Specialist Operations directorate. It is split into two parts: the Royalty and Specialist Protection (SO14) section, and the Parliamentary and Diplomatic Protection (PaDP).

The SO14 section provides armed officers to protect nominated members of the Royal Family, the Prime Minister and a select number of government ministers. These same officers also provide protection for all visiting foreign heads of state, as well as carrying out Close Protection, Residential Protection (at such locations as Buckingham Palace, Windsor Castle and Balmoral in Scotland), as well as Special Escort Group duties, which includes armed motorcycle riders. The section also provides Personal Protection Officers, who are highly trained individuals not only in the use of firearms, but advanced driving techniques, unarmed combat, and emergency first aid. They will also decide on the best route to take to a particular event, check out the venue before the principle arrives, and guard them while they are on site.

The Parliamentary and Diplomatic Protection (PaDP) unit, meanwhile, provides armed officers to protect high-profile buildings such as foreign embassies and consulates, as part of their responsibility under the Vienna Convention on Diplomatic Relations. It is also responsible for guarding the Palace of Westminster, including the Houses of Parliament and Downing Street, home to the Prime Minister and the Chancellor of the Exchequer.

The PaDP was formed as recently as April 2015, when the Diplomatic Protection Group (SO16) and the Palace of Westminster Division (SO17), amalgamated, although the Diplomatic Protection Group was originally formed in November 1974.

CHAPTER TWO

The Selection Process to Become a Police Firearms Officer

The opportunity to become a police Authorised Firearms Officer (AFO) is open to both male and female officers. There are two aspects to the role. The first is simple and straightforward: an officer must volunteer, except for in Northern Ireland, where it is compulsory. The second is a little more detailed and involves a perspective candidate reading through the detailed policy on the police's use of firearms as laid down by the College of Policing.

An officer cannot simply apply to become an AFO; they have to apply for a position on a unit, squad, or a firearms user group, who, as part of their policing role, require their officers to carry firearms for operational police purposes. This could be on a full-time basis, at an airport, for example, or as and when it is needed, such as on a surveillance unit. The officers on the latter of these two units (surveillance) would usually only carry a firearm for self-protection purposes.

Before an officer is even considered for a firearms course, there are three stages they must undertake. The first is a medical assessment. The second is a check of their disciplinary and driving records. If any officer's discipline record is ladened with complaints for aggressive related behaviour, or their driving record shows they have been involved in several police pursuit-related accidents, it might show that they are reckless by nature. If either were applicable then this would more than likely throw up a red flag, which would preclude the officer from being considered for an AFO. If they pass the first two stages, however, they must then undergo a firearm appraisal. This is essentially a role play scenario, where the officer will be given a brief outline of an incident, such as an armed robbery, where those responsible have escaped and have made their way to a location where the applicant will have to locate the individual and then deal with them in an appropriate manner. The ultimate purpose of the exercise is to see if the officer can remain calm under extreme pressure, whilst still being able to make a clear decision as to whether they can justifiably pull the trigger of their weapon.

As a former AFO with the Essex Police myself, I can easily recall my own firearm appraisal that I undertook back in 1988. Although I can't remember all these years later how I had been informed that my application had been successful, I do remember being told to attend a disused factory unit on an industrial estate in Basildon. We were provided with a set of black coveralls, a belt, holster, a Smith & Wesson revolver, and six blank rounds of ammunition. We were shown how to use the gun, which was basically aim and squeeze the trigger.

The story I was given was that there had been an armed robbery in Basildon town centre, where shots had been fired. Two men had made off from the scene and were now believed to be hiding somewhere in the factory's office area. I was then tasked with searching for the two men and dealing with whatever I came up against.

I started off by slowly walking along a corridor with offices either side of it. Each of the offices had a boarded bottom half and a frosted glass top half. Having never held a gun before, and knowing nothing about police firearms tactics, other than what I had seen in films, I decided to hold the gun in both hands. I have no idea why; it was just what I decided to do. I had gone about 20 yards when I came to a closed door on my left-hand side. Rather than simply taking my left hand off the gun and trying the door handle, I decided to maintain my stance and open the door with my right foot. I was, however, conscious not to stand immediately in front of it when I did. The door was unlocked and slowly popped open. It was hinged on its right-hand side, and I gently pushed it as wide open as it would go before it came to rest against a partition wall. Before I opened the door fully, I could clearly see there was nobody on either side or immediately behind it. The room was about 14 feet square with a large window occupying the far side. The main part of the room went off to the left, which then had another partition wall and another closed door in the middle of it.

I moved towards it and opened it in the same manner as I had with the main office door. It swung open, round to the right, and I could clearly see a man sat on the window ledge holding a large knife in his right hand. I must admit to being somewhat startled and nervous. I could feel my heartbeat rising, and although my brain kept telling me it was only a scenario, it suddenly became very real. This was also the point in time where I discovered if I could make my brain and mouth work in tandem with each other. The trick is to try to remain calm whilst at the same time taking effective control of the situation.

I believe the first thing I said, as I pointed my gun at the guy, was, 'Show me your hands,' which he did, only for me to notice a rather large knife in his right hand. Despite having no experience of such situations, my brain somehow allowed me to remain calm. 'OK, slowly get down off the window ledge and put your hands in the air.' Once again, he did what I asked him to. It was strange because what my inner self wanted to do was to scream and shout at this guy as loudly as I could, but I somehow managed not to. The guy then slowly started walking towards me, still holding the knife, but now he was talking and telling me in great detail what he was going to do to me with the knife. I had already decided that I was only prepared to back off as far as the main office door, and I also knew that there was going to come a time in the following thirty seconds or so that I was going to have to pull the trigger.

My natural inner self was telling me to keep the guy about 6 feet away from me: far enough for him not to be an immediate threat to me, but close enough so that I could remain in control of the situation.

The guy continued to walk towards me, but by now he was wielding the knife out to his right-hand side, still telling me what he was going to do to me with it. My brain was awash with what it wanted me to say, but I believe the best I managed to come out with was something like, 'Don't do anything that will make me have to pull the trigger.' I could have said anything, but it wouldn't have made the slightest difference to what the final outcome was always going to be. Finally, I had reached the doorway of the main office, which was as far as I was prepared to go. By now my commands to the guy were nothing more than a distant noise, as my heart rate rapidly increased. He took a further step towards me and I pulled the trigger. Not once, but twice.

'OK, stand down,' one of the instructors called out. 'How do you think that went?' I was asked. Without wanting to appear cocky, I replied, 'Not too bad, if I'm being honest. It certainly felt OK.' That was it. My scenario was over. Nothing further was said. No hint of how I had done was given to me by any of the instructors. What I didn't realise was that all of them, along with seven other officers who were also taking their appraisals, were all there in the room watching me. I didn't have a clue. I had just been so wrapped up in the scenario and what I was doing, I had been oblivious to them being there.

Two weeks later, I received a memo informing me I had passed and that I would be advised in due course when my basic firearms course would take place.

Perhaps at this stage it is worthwhile clarifying exactly what an AFO is: a police officer who has been selected, trained, accredited and authorised to carry a firearm operationally, by a chief officer of the individual's force. It does somehow appear to miss the fact that the starting point of this journey begins with the officer volunteering to carry out the role. This also means that the individual officer can determine to stop being an AFO at their own request. This could be for perfectly sensible reasons and even of a temporary nature due to personal reasons connected to a relationship breakup, for example, a family bereavement, or health concerns for themselves or one of their close family relatives. It could also simply be that they no longer wish to be an AFO and want to change roles, or because they have moved on due to having been promoted to another rank.

The policy is a generic one in so far as it relates to a number of different roles that a police officer might want to undertake whilst operating as an AFO. This might include being an officer of an Armed Response Vehicle, a Specialist Firearms Officer, or a Rifle Officer, more commonly referred by the officers as a 'Sniper'.

The thing to remember about policies such as these is that they are never straight forward, especially police-related ones. Indeed, they are not intended to be because they must cover a multitude of possibilities and eventualities. Above all else they include clarity for the officers about what is expected of them.

The following is a list of the skills issued by the College of Policing in the UK that AFOs are expected to have in order to carry out their roles effectively:

1. Good communication skills with the ability to listen to others.
2. The ability to produce concise statements or other documents.

3. To be skilled in the use of standard or user specific IT packages, systems and/or databases to fulfil role requirements.
4. The ability to use resources efficiently in their own role in accordance with procedures, policy and guidance.
5. The ability to identify potential opportunities to enhance efficiency and/or effectiveness within own area of work.
6. The ability to identify cause and effect and develop a course of action designed to target root causes and mitigate risks.
7. The ability to work effectively in a team to achieve shared objectives, demonstrating awareness of individual differences and providing support as required.
8. The ability to review their own performance objectively and to take steps to maintain and enhance competence.
9. To maintain professional standards appropriate to the role.
10. The ability to appropriately prioritise and plan their own work.
11. The ability to proactively develop effective working relationships with colleagues, partners and other stakeholders.
12. To be competent with a range of weapons and tactical equipment appropriate to the role.
13. To be competent in the provision of ballistic first aid.
14. To understand post deployment procedures.
15. The ability to act with discretion and emotional intelligence to manage conflict and defuse difficult situations.
16. The ability to apply procedures and legislation in line with policy and guidance.
17. The ability to respond appropriately to vulnerable persons.
18. To understand other armed policing roles.
19. To understand firearms, ammunition, ballistics, protection characteristics and capabilities.
20. To be competent in a range of tactical options commensurate with their AFO role(s).

Did you notice that the list of required skills reached point twelve before there was any mention of anything to do with the officer's use of, and ability with, firearms?

As if the required skill set with twenty separate requirements was not demanding enough, this is then layered with a list of what they are expected to do, known as Key Accountabilities:

1. Respond to conflict situations using a range of tactical options, assessing the threat to determine a proportionate response in line with legislation, policy and guidance.
2. Assess the immediacy and proximity of threat in order to make operational decisions for the protection of life.
3, Apply the National Decision Model to manage their response to a situation in a reasonable and proportionate way.
4. Justify the proportionate and lawful use of force in line with legal accountabilities.
5. Understand their role within the context of the wider police operation to support the achievement of operational strategies and priorities for action.
6. Gather and handle information and intelligence from a variety of sources, to assess threats in line with legislation, policies and guidance to take the appropriate action.
7. Provide public reassurance when deployed within communities.
8. Provide medical aid commensurate with training as required to preserve life.

This means that an officer now has a list of twenty-eight points they must comply with, and remember, before they even consider pulling the trigger of their weapon. On top of this there is a further list of what are called 'Competencies', of which there are six split into two levels, not one of which mentions the words firearms or guns.

1. We are emotionally aware – Level 1: Practitioner.
2. We take ownership – Level 1: Practitioner.
3. We collaborate – Level 1: Practitioner.
4. We support and inspire – Level 1: Practitioner.
5. We analyse critically – Level 2: Supervisor or middle manager.
6. We are innovative and open-minded – Level 1: Practitioner.

Having successfully understood all the technical requirements of the role, an officer must then successfully complete their basic firearms course before they can become an AFO. But that is not the end of their training, far from it. To ensure that officers maintain the required standard to retain their authority to carry a firearm for operational police purposes, and to continue in the role as an AFO, they have what is known as a Continuing Professional Development (CPD). This requires them to:

- Undertake mandatory refresher training in all modules and units of the National Police Firearms Training Curriculum (NPFTC) in accordance with, or relevant to the role.
- Undertake additional mandatory refresher training as determined by their force or agency.
- Annually meet health and fitness standards relevant to the role.

From a shooting aspect, officers must requalify three times a year by shooting at targets from different distances with a number of different weapons. These are called 'Qualification Shoots'. The required standard for an officer to retain their firearms permit is to score a minimum of 70%, although some forces require a 90% pass rate, the latter of which equates to successfully hitting the target forty-five times from fifty shots. The reality is that for every round an AFO fires that misses its intended target, an innocent member of the public could be hit and killed, meaning it is only right and proper that the required pass mark on a qualification shoot remains high.

Despite the inherent and obvious dangers that relate to being an AFO, other than the kudos of being a firearms officer, there are no obvious advantages that automatically come with the role, and certainly no additional financial increment – an AFO gets paid the same money as an officer walking the beat or driving round in a car.

CHAPTER THREE

Shooting and Tactics

A member of a police firearms unit must be proficient at both shooting and tactics, which take many hours of training and operational experience to become proficient at. There are some, however, who are either naturally a good shot, or just have an in-built tactical awareness, or sometimes even both.

Officers usually must be able to master at least two weapons: a side arm as well as some kind of semi-automatic, and a single-shot carbine. However, there is every possibility that if an officer is part of a firearms unit for ten years or so, then the weapons they start using when they first joined will not be the ones they finish with.

By way of example, when I began my firearms career in 1989, the weapons used by Essex Police at the time were the Smith & Wessen model 10, the .38 six-shot revolver and the .32 Ruger carbine. Yet by the time I had finished my stint as a member of the Tactical Firearms Group (TFG), the firearms had changed to a Beretta 92f, 9-mm handgun, which took a nine-round magazine, and a Heckler & Koch 9-mm semi-automatic carbine, which used fifteen-round magazines. One of the main advantages of the change in weapons was the speed with which an officer could reload his weapon, should the need ever arise.

During my time as a firearms officer, an AFO was anybody other than those who were members of the TFG. They would undergo firearms training once a month and would alternate between shooting one month and tactics the next. It was different for those who were members of the TFG, who trained for two days every month, with one day spent on the tactical aspects of the roll and the other on shooting.

The tactical aspect was always interesting because it was never the same. A tactical training day might consist of practising entering a house, factory, boat, train, or even open country searches. Shooting days were on a firing range, either indoors or outside. Each officer would have to shoot at a paper target attached to a wooden board from different distances, starting at 5 metres, and which would then increase to 7, 10, 15, 20, and 25 metres.

In those days, to maintain their authorisation to carry firearms for police operational purposes, officers had to requalify three times a year. This meant having to undergo a fifty-round shoot, which, combined with the different distances, also included an officer firing from different positions: standing, kneeling and prone, or laying down. Out of a fifty-round shoot, an officer had to hit the targets within the specified areas a total of forty-five times, or in other words, had to achieve a 95% pass rate. To some this might sound quite high, but it had to be like this because for every shot that misses the target, the reality is that on a live operation, it is a shot that sails off down the High Street and which then has the ability to hurt or kill an innocent member of the public. Not a positive outcome from anybody's perspective.

The tactics that were taught back in the 1990s in Essex were different to what they are today, with the TFG and the AFOs being taught to a different standard. This was mainly because AFOs, who were based on traffic and manned the Armed Response Vehicles, were the firearms officers initially sent to the scene of a firearms incident, in essence to 'hold the fort'. This could be seen as a rather strange decision, as any police force would surely want to send their best and most highly trained officers to be first on the scene of an incident, but that is how it was.

A police firearms unit would be split into several shifts so that at least one was always available to attend a firearms-related incident. This system also allowed for a shift to be on rest days or training days. Using Essex Police as an example, one shift worked an 8am to 4pm day, which allowed for them to be called in early to deal with any incidents that came in after 5am. They could also be kept on duty for up to two hours after their shift finished, but the rule of thumb was that firearms officers would not be deployed for any longer than twelve hours continuously. Another shift would then work from 10am until 6pm, and they too could be called in prior to the start of their intended shift and kept on after they were due to finish. A third shift worked from 6pm until 2am, although on a Sunday this was changed to 4pm to midnight (also referred to as a 'half-night'). If they had finished their shift and gone home, they were usually the first ones to be called out if an incident came in up until about 5am. However, such a decision was job dependent and was not set in stone.

The problem with having to call a shift back to work is that its members lived all over the county. The Force Support Unit (FSU) office back in the 1990s was located within the headquarters complex in Chelmsford. The shift I was a member of included officers who lived in Colchester (23 miles/33 minutes travelling time), Harlow (20 miles/38 minutes travelling time), Southend (21 miles/38 minutes travelling time) and Basildon (19 miles/27 minutes travelling). This meant that by the time all the officers had arrived in the office and collected their firearms from the armoury, as well as all their personal equipment, and had then travelled to either the scene of the incident or the nearest police station to it, more than an hour would have passed since the officers had been called in. Before they could be deployed to the scene, the officers would need be briefed about the incident and then allocated their jobs in the team as part of the overall operation. Add to this the time it took between the incident having been reported to the police and the decision made to request firearms officers, and it could quite easily be more than two hours since the original incident had begun.

In Essex, each firearms team consisted of what was known as a Raid Team and a Support Team. The Raid Team consisted of a Raid 1 (R1) and a Raid 2 (R2). The Support Team consisted of a Support 1 (S1) with the rest of the officers not having specifically allocated titles. The R1 and R2 would determine the direction of the search, whilst the S1 was the link between the Raid Team and the Support Team. They would have to try to second guess which way the R1 and R2 would carry out their search, and have any necessary equipment to hand, such as ladders, mirrors or torches, which they assumed the Raid Team might need. The S1 also had to know when to call up another member of the Support Team to provide cover when it was needed at any given time during a search. Although rare, an S1 might also need to momentarily stop the Raid Team from progressing further with their search whilst equipment or personnel had reached their required locations, or if he simply felt they were moving too fast and, by doing so, were over stretching the team.

Although this was the system I was trained in and was how numerous operations played out, the one niggling question I always had in the back of my mind was 'what if?' It had crossed my mind on more than one occasion that there was the possibility, however unlikely, that either one, or both, of the Raid Team might be shot during an operation whilst searching a premises. If this scenario did unfold and there were no other Raid-trained officers who were part of the team, what would happen then? Who would take over the search? There was also the added issue of having a 'man down', because it might not have been possible to reach them to discover if they were alive or dead, or to retrieve their body. This was not an eventuality that was considered or trained for, certainly not during my experience as a firearms officer. Common sense dictates that the only sensible option would have been to back off and contain the situation until suitable personnel were available, which is most definitely not an ideal position to be in.

There were occasions during a firearms operation when the decision was taken to simply go and knock on the front door of a property to arrest a particular individual. At such times, an armoured vehicle was usually used for cover. Despite officers aiming their firearms directly at the suspect, there were many occasions when the S1 would not even draw their own firearm, because more often than not, they would first place their hands on the detained individual and either search and handcuff them, or immediately hand them over to other members of the support team to deal with. The latter option would definitely be the case if there was more than one suspect in the house.

Although there was a set way of doing things, with the safety of the officers always being paramount, things do not always go according to plan and when that happens, officers must think on their feet and be quick about it. A matter of seconds could mean the difference between life and death. I remember a few instances I was personally involved in when the execution of the operation did not quite go according to plan.

Sometime back in the early 1990s, three men were wanted for a number of armed robberies carried out against unsuspecting members of the public in their north-Essex homes. On each occasion the occupants had been threatened with a handgun.

Information had been gathered identifying the men and the car they were using to commit the robberies. The incident in question ended up with the car being stopped on a major A road somewhere in the north of the county. I can't remember exactly how this happened but can only assume that the individuals concerned had been under surveillance and had been seen driving away and arrangements had been made for us to intercept and arrest them.

Twelve officers, all of whom were armed, set off in three unmarked police cars. The plan was textbook and straight forward. The three police vehicles would locate the suspect's car, box it in and then put into operation what is referred to as a 'hard stop'. In essence, the first police vehicle gets ahead of the suspect and begins to slow its speed down. The second police vehicle drives immediately behind it, and the third vehicle pulls alongside it. When the command is given to 'strike', all three police vehicles stop, leaving the offending vehicle no other option but to stop as well. What is then supposed to happen is the police officer in the rear nearside of the police vehicle that has pulled up immediately alongside the suspect's car, throws in a challenge whilst aiming his firearm at the suspects. Whilst the officer is doing that, the other three officers are supposed to get out of the vehicle on the offside, providing them with good bullet proof cover, before they take over challenging the suspect. This then allows the police officer who had originally begun the challenge from inside the vehicle to join his colleagues on the offside of their vehicle. From that position, each of the occupants of the suspect's vehicle are then instructed to get out, one at a time, before being arrested.

What happened on this occasion was slightly different. Everything went like clockwork up to the point of the 'strike'. The officer in the rear nearside passenger seat (me) threw in a loud and aggressive verbal challenge to the startled occupants of the suspect's vehicle, whilst at the same pointing my Heckler & Koch MP5 carbine towards them, using a small ballistic shield for my own protection just in case I was fired upon. The driver of the vehicle and the rear offside passenger alighted from the police vehicle as they should have, and took up their offensive positions, but this was where it went slightly wrong. Instead of climbing out through the front offside door, the front nearside passenger simply opened his door right on to the suspect's vehicle and started challenging them. This placed the rear nearside passenger (me) in a bit of a predicament but, thinking on my feet and momentarily putting the correct way of conducting the operation to one side, and whilst still aiming my MP5 at the individual's vehicle, I also opened my door, got out and started challenging the individual sat in the rear offside of the suspect's vehicle. The car was quickly surrounded by the other armed officers present and the three suspects were all arrested on suspicion of aggravated burglary. No firearms were recovered from inside the vehicle.

If any members of the public, or divisional, uniformed police officers had witnessed the stop, they would have been impressed because what took place was impactive, decisive, nobody was hurt, all the suspects were arrested, and, overall, it looked very professional. As for the firearms officers who carried out the operation, they all recognised the obvious mistake, but the main thing was that once things had gone slightly away from the intended plan, the officers acted quickly, adapting the best way that they could. They got the job done and at the end of the day, everybody returned home safely to their families. A conversation subsequently took place between the front seat passenger, me, and the other two occupants of the police vehicle. The following morning, the officer concerned appeared in the office with a large number of cream cakes. His fine was paid, and a lesson had been duly learnt.

In the early 1990s I remember another armed robbery that had taken place on a building society in north Essex. Enquiries by local detectives quickly discovered the name of the suspect and where they lived, which was a local address. After a briefing at the local police station, three unmarked police vehicles containing twelve TFG members, all dressed in plain clothes, drove to the suspect's address, which was a ground floor maisonette. There was no way of accessing the rear of the premises, so it was a case of getting to the front door as quickly as possible, which was some way back from the road, maybe as far as 25 yards. As four officers approached the front door, two of us knocked whilst the other two took aim with their MP5 carbines at a large bay window immediately to the right of the door. The knock did not illicit an immediate response, so the two officers tried again. There was no reply the second time, but an elderly female figure suddenly appeared in the window, only to see two armed police officers aiming their firearms at her. She made her way to the front door and opened it. One of the officers took hold of her arm and gently pulled her towards him, asking if the person we were looking for was in the property. She said that nobody of that name lived there, and there was a moment's confusion amongst my fellow officers because the elderly lady was clearly telling the truth. The same officer then described the person to her. 'Oh, you mean young Gary,' she exclaimed. 'Yes, that's him,' the officer said. 'He lives there, 97a,' she said, pointing at the front door of the adjoining downstairs maisonette. It was a quick about turn. The officers wasted no time in knocking on the door of the property, and the wanted man answered the door only to be immediately confronted by four rather large police officers aiming guns at him. Before any of the officers uttered a single word, he had his hands in the air, offered absolutely no resistance, and was quickly arrested.

When the incident's debrief took place back at the local police station, it turned out that the detective who had obtained the information about the suspect had simply made a mistake and had informed us that the address we wanted was 97 rather than the correct address of 97a. It is such small margins like this that can make all the difference. When the suspect was later interviewed, he told the detectives that he had not been aware of the commotion going on at his neighbour's address until he heard a knock on his own front door. The operation had a positive outcome, but could have been so different, all because of the slightest of administrative errors.

There were several humorous incidents that I can recall taking place during my time as a firearms officer, but one in particular comes readily to mind. Once again it was in the early 1990s and involved the protection of an individual at their home, who at the time was considered to be a very important person. There were two aspects of this story that are worthy of mention. Firstly, members of the firearms unit had arrived at the individual's home just after 6pm one evening to provide security for a prominent individual and their family, only to find a live .762 round of ammunition on the driveway. The tension amongst the police officers rose noticeably after the find, especially after a rudimentary check proved that it was not a brand of bullet used by Essex Police riflemen. It was never discovered where the round had come from or who had dropped it there.

The second part of the story was that on this particular evening, the prominent individual and their partner had gone out, but there were still other family members in the property. When the couple returned, one of them had clearly consumed copious amounts of alcohol and proceeded to make a few suggestive comments towards one of the officers. None of the armed officers, despite their surprise, said a single word in reply. The partner of the person concerned was far from happy, but rather than berate them, they attempted to try to chastise the officer who had been the subject of the suggestive comments. The situation came to an abrupt end when it was politely suggested to the individual that they might like to take their unlocked red parliamentary box with them before going to bed.

The police and the use of firearms went through a big change in its approach towards its officer's overt appearance whilst armed. Prior to Desert Storm during the First Gulf War in 1991, whenever a police officer was carrying a firearm, the weapon had to be hidden from view of the general public. Even on a scorching hot day, if an officer was carrying a firearm it had to be covered by a jacket. In Essex, all of this changed on 17 January 1991, when Desert Storm saw British and Allied forces put troops on the ground in Kuwait in their efforts to expel the occupying Iraqi forces.

The old Stansted Airport, which today is just the business area of the airport, was all that previously existed. What was not known to the general public at the time was that Stansted had been designated by the government as the location where all British casualties, wounded or otherwise, would be brought back to the UK. Consequently, Essex Police firearms officers were overtly armed for the first time at such a location, whilst conducting what in essence was a routine patrol at an airport. A photograph exists of two members of Essex Police carrying out an armed patrol in the airport's main concourse. One of the officers in the photograph is me. Never again did Essex Police officers have to conceal their weapons whist conducting foot patrols at Stansted. This more reasoned and realistic approach made total sense, because if somebody was intending to commit a terrorist attack, there is every possibility that they would do some kind of dry run first, a recce, so they could decide the best way to carry out such an act. If they saw that security was on a high level of alert, along with large numbers of armed police officers walking round the airport, it might just make them think twice about what they were planning to do.

This also highlighted the numerous different tactical scenarios police firearms officers had to train for. An armed suspect was the great unexpected. They might be on foot, in a car, in a house, flat, bungalow or large business premises, a wooded area, a shopping centre, an aeroplane or even an airport. Each of these locations required a slightly different tactical approach, especially if it allowed for large numbers of members of the public to congregate in.

Pulling the trigger of a gun is easy, something that anybody can do, but doing it for real when the target you are aiming at is a living, breathing human being might not be so easy for some. It is enough to make an officer stop and think for a split second, a moment in time that might just be long enough for them, or one of their colleagues, to be shot and killed, but where it is possible for the tactics to play out as they were planned, then nobody has to be in a position where they even have to consider pulling the trigger in the first place.

CHAPTER FOUR

Public Perception

The main reason why British police officers throughout England, Scotland and Wales are not routinely armed as they go about their day-to-day duties is simply because they never have been.

When the Metropolitan Police was formed by John Peel back in the early nineteenth century, the general public's major concern was that in real terms, this new force would end up being some kind of paramilitary extension of the British Army and simply become just another oppressive arm of the government. There was also the risk that by arming this new force, the public's trust and support in it would be immediately undermined.

Peel's 'sale' of this new body of law enforcement officers to the general public had been based on the principle that its main duty was to help protect and keep them safe, and not to impose the will of the state. It was the beginning of policing by consent. This was a time when the common man and woman simply wanted a better life for themselves and their families but were constantly kept down by the upper classes who had absolute control in all government affairs. Any previous strike, rebellion or public show of unrest had usually been met by the government with brute force, which usually came in the form of the army being deployed on British streets.

As well as deciding that his new group of men would not routinely carry firearms, Peel also determined what colour their uniform should be. He specifically wanted to avoid red, which at the time was the colour of the tunic worn by the British Army. He certainly put a lot of thought into what he was doing with these newly formed police Constables, or 'Peelers' as they were more affectionately known by the public.

Early policing was not entirely bereft of the use of firearms, but they were not worn on a daily basis. They were available when the need arose and then only to Constables who had knowledge and experience of their use.

For readers who grew up with TV in the 1960s and 1970s, one of the programmes available to watch was the BBC's *Dixon of Dock Green*. The series ran for twenty-one years from 1955 to 1976 and focused on everyday policing at a fictional London police station, with the star of the show being a character called Sergeant George Dixon. An officer of a more 'mature' age, he dealt with all the situations that arose with care, compassion, sympathy and understanding. In essence, he was there to help rather than be archaic and dictatorial.

Thanks to this programme, two generations of the British public grew up watching Sergeant George Dixon and his colleagues dealing with people and incidents as fairly as they could, always with the public's best interests at heart. Seeing Dixon appearing every week on TV looking resplendent in his uniform and chin-strapped helmet created an image in the minds of millions of people of how they believed policing was, and how it should be. Out of the hundreds of episodes broadcast, only a few contained incidents involving a requirement for the police to use firearms, all of which were in keeping with the reason for their issue, something which was readily understood by the viewers.

Having said all of that, it would be somewhat naïve to believe that in certain circumstances, police officers were not issued with firearms from time to time, when it was necessary to protect members of the public, or themselves, from armed criminals. Capital punishment throughout Britain was not suspended until 1965, and still remained as a punishment for certain offences, such as treason, until 1998, which in part meant that before then, anybody using a firearm to kill somebody had nothing to lose by also trying to shoot the policemen trying to capture them, making such a scenario extremely dangerous for unarmed officers.

Over time, the British public have become more accustomed to seeing police officers routinely carrying firearms at locations such as airports, Downing Street, Buckingham Palace, and foreign embassies, especially since the terrorist attacks on the Twin Towers in New York on 11 September 2001, but not whilst officers are on routine patrol.

The other aspect of the equation is of course the officers themselves. Most of them do not want to be routinely armed. For many, making decisions in day-to-day policing can be stressful and difficult enough, so the thought of having to carry a gun and ultimately having to potentially make split-second, life-threatening decisions is simply not for them.

If British police forces ever took the decision to arm all of their officers, they would have to plan for it years in advance to ensure that they had a sufficient number of officers who were willing to carry a firearm, and that those individuals were then of the required calibre to do so. There would have to be a major decline in the nation's social fabric before any of the country's Chief Constables would be bold enough to make the call to permanently arm all their officers.

There is certainly something about a police officer carrying a firearm that makes it less likely that they will be approached by member of the public, especially if they have a machine gun strapped across their chest.

One of the relevant issues surrounding the subject of seeing armed police officers on the streets of Britain is that of the public perception. If a firearms-related incident takes place, most members of the public would understand and recognise the need and justification for the deployment of police officers carrying firearms. Most people accept seeing heavily armed police officers patrolling around the nation's airports as it has become normalised over the years, but when this same scenario occurs on the streets or in a shopping centre, it produces a different reaction.

If police officers are carrying firearms, then this is always for a reason, which in nearly every case is to protect the public from an actual, or perceived threat of an individual or group, who is, or has been, seen either carrying a firearm or weapon that could seriously injure or kill somebody. The problem arises when members of the public see police officers carrying firearms as part of their everyday duties and they do not know the reason why. The irony in these situations is that despite the fact they are there to either reassure and protect the public from a potential threat, it can quite often have the opposite effect and can cause uncertainty, anxiety, and even panic, simply because it is just not something the British public, on the whole, are used to seeing. Unlike many countries throughout Europe, South America, the United States, Australia, and Canada, where police officers are routinely armed, that is not the case throughout the United Kingdom, nor is it true in countries such as Norway, Iceland, Ireland and New Zealand, to name but a few.

I remember an incident one day when three colleagues and I were in a marked police vehicle driving in the Thurrock area of Essex, when a car passed us on the near side and a rear passenger in the vehicle thought he was being clever when he laughed and made a rude gesture to us with his right hand. The driver of the police vehicle activated his blue lights and caused the vehicle to stop. What the young man hadn't seen, and couldn't have possibly known, was that me and my three colleagues were in fact all wearing 9-mm side arms. There were three young men in the car, two in the front and one on the back of the vehicle, and once they saw the guns, there was no laughing, no smiling, only silence. The two in the front had been unaware of what their 'friend' in the rear had done to cause the vehicle to be stopped, but that didn't stop all three of them from being arrested, however, because a quantity of cannabis was found, although none of them would admit to whom it belonged. To add insult to injury, the man behind the wheel of the car was also a disqualified driver, which also meant he had no insurance. What was interesting, however, was how the demeanour of the man in the rear of the vehicle in particular totally changed once he saw we were carrying firearms.

People usually think of the United States or countries in Europe when they think of police carrying firearms, and certainly when it comes to the former there is a belief that the arming of police forces is in keeping with how violent the country is perceived to be. In essence, the rise in the number of deployments of police officers using firearms is generally a reaction to the times we now find ourselves living in. In recent years there has been a marked increase in terror attacks throughout Britain and Europe, as well as a marked rise in acts of serious violent crime.

For all police officers who carry firearms as part of their roll, no matter where they are, it really is a case of walking the thin blue line. Despite what people may or may not think, police officers do not want to carry a gun because they want to shoot somebody; this is the last thing they want to do and is the furthest thing from their minds.

Whenever a police officer discharges their firearm and kills somebody, there is always the possibility they could end up facing a murder or manslaughter charge. It is only right and proper that they are accountable for their actions, but the pressure they are under is immense. Quite often they will have a split second to make a decision that could end up costing somebody their life, whilst at the same time greatly affecting their own and that of their family.

The hope for police officers when they confront an armed criminal is that the person sees the fire power they are up against and immediately puts down their weapon, realising that resistance to what they are being confronted with is futile, and that their only option is to lay down their arms and surrender.

CHAPTER FIVE

Authorised Firearms Officers – AFOs

There are only five forces throughout the United Kingdom where all officers routinely carry firearms as part of their everyday duties. In no particular order these are: the Police Service of Northern Ireland, the Belfast Harbour Police, Belfast International Airport Constabulary, the Ministry of Defence Police, and the Civil Nuclear Constabulary.

All these forces, and all other firearms officers in whichever force area they work in, regardless of what standard they are trained to, are first and foremost an AFO. This means they are police officers who are trained and authorised to carry firearms for police operational purposes. It is a universal term that is used by all police forces throughout the UK and was adopted due to reforms brought in after the January 1983 shooting of Stephen Waldorf by Metropolitan Police detectives in London. These same reforms also standardised the nationwide training for officers wishing to be AFOs, as well as the rank an officer had to hold to allow them to authorise the issuing of firearms for operational purposes. The only exemption for the need to authorise officers to carry firearms on an operation-to-operation basis were for those officers permanently deployed on duties such guarding foreign embassies or government buildings, such as the Prime Minister's residence at 10 Downing Street, or those deployed as bodyguards for designated government officials or members of the Royal Family.

By 2020, the latest year that figures are available for, there was a total of 6,518 qualified AFOs throughout England, Scotland and Wales, which was just under 5% of the nation's serving police officers.

As has been previously mentioned, all AFOs are volunteers, and it is every officer's decision to want to carry a firearm and is not something that is forced upon them. Once an officer has decided they wish to become an AFO, they must undergo an in-depth selection process which differs slightly from force to force. The first part of it is having their initial application to undertake such training approved by a senior officer who works within the same policing division as they do.

When I first applied to be transferred to the Force Support Unit, which undertook all firearms operations within the Essex Police, a Chief Inspector wrote the following on my application: 'Do we really want somebody who is as childish and immature as this officer being allowed to progress to the FSU? It is not something which will necessarily reflect well on this division.'

These comments were based on the Chief Inspector having seen me laughing and joking as I went about my normal divisional duties; attributes the Chief Inspector did not care for. Fortunately for me, my Inspector informed the reluctant Chief Inspector that I had already held a firearms permit as an AFO for more than a year, and my application was approved without any further ado.

An officer must then undergo a medical examination to ensure they are physically fit enough to be a firearms officer. Next follows a fitness test, another test to check the applicant's psychological state of mind, an interview, and then finally, an assessment day where the applicant is put through a firearms-type scenario, which in essence is to see if the officer actually has the ability to pull the trigger.

Once an officer has got this far, they must then carry out their basic firearms course. Pass that and they become an AFO, but that is not the end of it. To keep their firearms authorisation, they must pass regular refresher training in both tactics and shooting to ensure that they are still up to the required standard. Fall short of this, and their firearms authorisation will be withdrawn.

Regardless of their level of training, all officers who carry firearms for operational police purposes are referred to as AFOs. However, in addition to this an officer can qualify as an Armed Response Vehicle Officer (ARVO), a Specialist Firearms Officer (SFO), and a Counter Terrorist Specialist Firearms Officer (CTSFO).

Armed Response Vehicles (ARVs) are operated by all police forces throughout the UK and are designed to be the initial response to any and all firearms incidents, those that are believed to involve the use of a firearm, or other potentially life-threatening implement, or where a person's life has or is being threatened. ARVs are police vehicles that have been adapted to carry firearms and other specialist equipment, although a number of forces have given their ARV officers a standing authority to carry their sidearms openly. The then Commissioner of the Metropolitan Police, Sir Paul Condon, first issued this standing authority in May 1994, although ARVs had been deployed in the capital since 1991. The Greater Manchester Police did the same in September that same year, and the Chief Constable of Police Scotland made the similar decision in 2013. However, the original idea behind ARVs first came about as a result of the West Yorkshire Police who, back in 1976, deployed what they called 'instant response cars', which contained two officers with firearms in an internal safe.

In my time of carrying out ARV duties, the weapons used by Essex Police were the 9-mm Beretta 92f semi-automatic pistol, and the 9-mm Heckler & Koch MP5 semi-automatic Carbine. At the time it was seen as an added bonus that both weapons used the same ammunition. Most forces upgraded their weaponry in 2010, replacing the Beretta handgun with several different options, including the Glock 17 semi-automatic handgun, whilst the Heckler & Kock MP5 was replaced with more powerful weapons such as the Heckler & Koch G36C 5.56-mm carbine. This change came about because of the worldwide terrorist threat that was on the increase from the early 2000s, and it is the Chief Constable and the police authority of each force who ultimately decide which firearms their own officers will be issued with.

In September 2014, in response to a Freedom of Information request by a member of the public, Essex Police stated that they used the following weapons for operational purposes at that time:

    Accuracy International Bolt Action Rifle
    Tikka T3 Bolt Action Rifle
    H&K 417 Semi-Automatic Rifle
    H&K G36C Carbine
    H&K L1004A2 Launcher (Baton Gun)
    Sig Pro Self-Loading Pistol
    Sig P250 Self-Loading Pistol
    Benelli Nova/Super Nova Pump Shotgun
    TASER

It is common practice for all ARV vehicles to have a specific identification mark on their roofs so that they are readily identifiable to police helicopters, which is especially useful during fluid and fast-moving firearm-related operations, where time is all important.

Specialist Firearms Officer (SFO)

An SFO is an officer who has undergone training to a more advanced level than a standard AFO. SFOs receive additional training in areas such as building interventions and tactics. Their primary function is entering different types of premises looking for armed and dangerous criminals, hard vehicle stops, armed sieges, undertaking high-risk firearms related arrests, and, in more recent years, responding effectively and rapidly to terrorist-type scenarios. An SFO today would have been the equivalent to a TFG member back in my time as a firearms officer.

Counter Terrorist Specialist Firearms Officer (CTSFO)

A CTSFO is the most highly trained firearms officers a police force has in its armoury and deals with all firearms incidents up to and including a terrorist threat. This level of police firearms response was specifically established by the Metropolitan Police in the build-up to the London 2012 Summer Olympic Games. These units were set up in several forces throughout the UK, and because of the uniformity of the training provided, part of which included input from UK's Special Forces, standardised procedures and weaponry, CTSFOs are able to work in conjunction with other police forces should a terrorist-related incident arise.

With acts of terrorism having increased in the years since the 9/11 attacks in New York in 2001, it was recognised that there would be a need to increase the number of police officers involved in CTSFO work, and so the Home Office instigated the National Armed Uplift Programme in 2016. Part of this was the CTSFO uplift project, a two-year recruitment drive to encourage more officers to volunteer for the type of work undertaken by CTSFO units. This proved to be an extremely successful initiative, and in 2019, the National Police Chiefs' Council announced an increase in CTSFO numbers of 63%.

Having decided to embark on a career in firearms and be deemed good enough to be issued with a police firearms permit for operational purposes, an officer then has to take into account the legal mine field which comes hand in hand with their chosen career path in policing.

From a policing aspect, officers must consider the Code of Practice on Police use of Firearms and Less Lethal Weapons issued by the Home Office, and the Association of Chief Police Officers (ACPO) *Manual of Guidance on Police Use of Firearms*. As if that wasn't enough to contend with, officers must then consider certain elements of the Police and Criminal Evidence Act 1984, along with the Human Rights Act 1998.

The legal situation in the UK means that police officers are only allowed to use reasonable force to carry out an arrest and to prevent a crime from taking place, or to protect themselves or others. If the reasonable force used results in a fatality, then the European Convention of Human Rights states that 'The use of force that can be used is no more than is absolutely necessary'. That judgement will of course differ from officer to officer, who will perceive events differently and react at a different speed. The ultimate test of whether they were right or wrong in their decision-making process could well be determined in court, where they will have to justify the actions they took in just a matter of seconds. A decision which could end up having far reaching ramifications for the rest of their life.

Out of all the policing areas throughout the UK, the force with by far the biggest number of firearms officers is the Metropolitan Police in London, with more than 2,500. Although this might sound like a lot, the number is from a workforce of 33, 972 as of 30 April 2024, or approximately 7%.

CHAPTER SIX

A Personal Insight into Life as a Police Firearms Officer

I spent thirty years serving as an officer with Essex Police, nine of which were spent working as an Authorised Firearms Officer (AFO), so I would like to take this opportunity to offer my personal experiences, based on my involvement in a large number of firearms incidents.

I joined Essex Police in 1983 and after five years of being a uniformed officer, performing general police duties, I applied to become an AFO. I had no prior experience of firearms, nor had I ever touched or even held a gun. When I was a serving police officer, it was normal practice that once our two-year probationary period had been successfully reached, we would then gain a few more years' experience of basic 'coppering', before going on to specialise in a preferred field of policing. The options were varied and included, in no particular order, promotion, traffic, becoming a detective on CID, a dog handler, a scene of crime forensics officer, or the Force Support Unit (FSU), which undertook firearms operations, dealt with all major public disorder incidents (whether that was policing a football match or a fox hunt), the diving unit, surveillance operations, and house-to-house enquiries for all major incidents such as murders, rapes, or terrorist situations. The FSU was formed in March 1973, with a strength of thirty-one officers. Its first Chief Inspector was Geoffrey Markham, who in 1984 became the Assistant Chief Constable of Essex Police, a position he held until his retirement in 1999 after forty-two years of service. There were also other units such as major crime, or the drugs squad, but they usually required you to become an experienced CID officer before you could be considered for such a position. Over time, other units that specialised in dealing with domestic violence, family liaison, or child abuse also became an everyday part of policing, but once again, officers who performed these roles also had several years of CID experience behind them.

It was the variation of different roles the FSU undertook that appealed to me. The never knowing what you would be doing, or where you would be, were the main draws; firearms just happened to be one of those roles.

Having successfully passed my firearm appraisal, I underwent a basic firearms course in Chelmsford in late 1988, which focused on gun handling, shooting ability and tactical awareness. This lasted for a period of six weeks and was on a pass or fail basis. If the instructors collectively felt one of the students was struggling in a particular aspect of the course, at any time, that was it. The course was over.

For someone to be told their desire to become a firearms officer is over must have been hard to accept, but that was how it had to be for both the student and Essex Police. Being a firearms officer is not for everybody. Some people are simply not cut out to deal with the type of pressure that comes with the role, whilst others are either not good enough shots or do not have the required tactical awareness.

Having passed the course and acquired my firearms permit, I returned to general police duties as a constable working out of Pitsea police station, where I became a divisional firearms officer. For the following ten months, I was only deployed twice in this role, once at a job in Pitsea and the other at Thundersley, both times working alongside members of the FSU's Tactical Firearms Group, who were looking for 'armed besieged criminals', individuals the police had been informed had threatened somebody, and at the time had either been in possession of a firearm or had claimed to have been in possession of one.

In September 1989, aged 25, I was successful in securing a position as an AFO on an FSU shift of the Essex Police, which at the time conducted all police firearms operations within the county, as well as dealing with all major public order incidents. They also conducted county-wide covert surveillance operations against high-value criminal targets.

This was somewhat of a strange transition for me, because after six years of policing, I suddenly found myself starting out all over again; a new boy on a unit of experienced individuals, and, it also has to be said, some very big characters. I wasn't exactly a wilting wall flower myself, but there was an accepted way of conducting oneself. The order of the day was to sit back, keep your mouth shut, observe what was going on, listen, take everything in and learn. To adopt what might be seen as a more robust, in your face, approach to the day-to-day internal workings of the unit would not have seen anybody remain in place for long.

There was definitely a pecking order in the group. It was a unit of experienced individuals who were certainly not backwards in coming forwards, so if someone had something to say, they said it. Nothing was held back, but nothing was said in a nasty way. There just wasn't the time to be all nice and fluffy, tell people what they might want to hear, or worry that they might be upset or offended by hearing somebody else's truth. If somebody made a mistake, got something wrong, forgot a piece of equipment or didn't pass on an important message, they needed to be told about it. To do so wasn't malicious, it was called learning. Thankfully, everybody understood that and just moved on.

The pecking order also saw a divide between certain members of the TFG in their attitude towards those members of the FSU who were only AFOs. Over a period of a few months during the early 1990s, the FSU had to carry out a long-term protection and welfare operation involving certain individuals who lived in different locations across the county. On one particular day of this operation, and with the day's pairings having been selected, I was crewed up with an experienced, long-standing member of both the FSU and the TFG. The particular individual on whom we were to conduct a welfare check lived in the very far reaches of northern Essex, and just to get to where they lived was more than a two-hour drive. On arrival, we were politely invited in, and a conversation ensued over a couple of cups of tea and a few biscuits. The welfare checks complete, we climbed back into our vehicle and began the return journey back to the FSU office at HQ in Chelmsford. We returned our firearms to the force armoury and made our way up to the office. We had been in each other's company for nearly six hours, and not one word had been spoken between us. Not one. From my perspective, as the junior officer in every aspect, I adopted the old school approach of 'speak when you're spoken to', and as my colleague never uttered a single word to me for the entire day, it was one of the quietest days I'd ever experienced as a member of the FSU.

There was one particular character, whom we shall call 'Petal', who let's just say wouldn't have been somebody's first choice to pick a fight with. Each morning there would usually be two shifts on duty at the same time, sometimes even three if the divers were on duty as well. One group started at 8am the other at 10pm, and the divers started as and when they needed to, depending on what they were doing. There would be occasions when there would be in the region of about thirty individuals sitting round a table in the parade room, having numerous conversations over a cup of tea or coffee. The trick was not to make eye contact with Petal because if you did, you had to take part in that morning's arm punching contest. On one particular morning, I made that very mistake but was fortunate enough to be the one delivering the first punch as the two of us faced off against each other. I hit a beauty of a strike on the top of his right arm and the grimace on Petal's face let the baying crowd known it had done its job. Every one of them raised their arms in the air as if in recognition that the beast had been slain, and the I mimicked their act of celebration. But Petal had clearly taken me raising my arms in front of his face as the defensive actions of a boxer and threw his own punch, which went straight between my slightly outstretched arms and caught me square on the chin. My left leg wobbled slightly but thankfully, the other held firm and I managed to stay on my feet. A shake of hands followed between us, and everybody returned to the table to finish off their drinks before carrying on with the day's respective duties.

When I arrived at the FSU, it consisted of just three women. There had been others before that who had already come and gone, and others came along afterwards, and at one point the Inspector in charge of the Weapons Training department was a female officer as well. There was always plenty of banter, whether that was in the office, whilst out on operations or training, but it was the same no matter who was present and was never specifically directed towards female officers. There was a camaraderie enjoyed amongst FSU members, which was hard to replicate anywhere else in policing, as individuals literally had to put their lives in the hands of their colleagues. They had to trust a command, instruction, order, or request without question, knowing that the person who had made it did so in the complete confidence and knowledge that it was safe to do so.

After successfully completing my Tactical Firearms Group (TFG) course, in the summer of 1990 I became a member of 'C' shift FSU, where I remained for the following eight extremely interesting and eventful years, during which time I took part in more than

100 firearm deployments. I chose to leave the FSU for personal reasons in 1997. I had separated from my wife about two years earlier, but we had joint custody of our two young sons, who spent one week living with their mother and the following week living with me. This continued on a weekly, rotating basis, but the longer it went on the more difficult it became for me to continue working on the FSU. If I was on a day shift, which meant having to drive from Basildon to Chelmsford, or I was called in early, I would quickly have to wake the boys, get them dressed and then drive them across town to my mother's house, which meant that not only did she then have to give them their breakfast, but she also had to walk them to school, which was about 2 miles away from where she lived. There were also many occasions where my mother had to collect them from school when I was involved in a firearms operation and was still at work. It was a reluctant decision for me to leave the FSU and put in a request to be posted to my hometown of Basildon, but from a family life perspective, it was the right decision. My sons were growing up quickly, years that once they had passed, were gone for ever. Being a member of the FSU was something I'd loved doing, but I loved my sons more and had no regrets about what I'd done.

The police use of firearms is a topic which is scrutinised closely by both the press and members of the public, especially if incident has resulted in somebody being shot. This understandably leads to the question whether the scenario could have been dealt with in a different way, which includes the overall management of the incident and if the individual concerned could have been dealt with by non-lethal methods. Having said that, there will never be a one fits all response, simply because by the very nature of these scenarios, different individuals are involved, as are the different types of weapons and the level of threat being displayed. Clearly, there would be absolutely no point in firing a TASER at an individual who is wearing a suicide vest, but it might be appropriate if the same individual were topless and carrying a knife.

The outcome of any scenario where the police feel the need to deploy firearms officers is always going to differ depending on the level of threat being posed by the individual concerned, which includes their mental state, their choice of weaponry and the perception of the threat being faced by the officers dealing with the incident.

There is no civilian-based role that requires an individual to carry a firearm, to have the ability to stay calm under extreme pressure, whilst at the same time still managing to be an effective resource, like a police firearms officer has to. Neither do they then have to consider pulling the trigger, shooting somebody, regardless of the circumstances. If the person they have shot subsequently dies, the firearms officer could then be facing a murder charge, which, if found guilty, could result in a sentence of life imprisonment.

Potentially, every time a firearms officer draws their weapon or has to aim it at another person, they may well have to pull the trigger, otherwise there would be no need to take such a course of action. Pull the trigger too early or too late and somebody might die unnecessarily. I found myself in that position on more than one occasion, but thankfully never had to pull the trigger. However, during the hi-jacking incident at Stansted Airport in 1996 (see Chapter Twenty-Two), I was part of the team tasked with arresting the terrorists as they came off the aircraft. Afterwards, we then had to go and search the plane, not knowing if other terrorists were still waiting for us on board. To say I was focused would be an understatement, and my finger did not leave the trigger for the entirety of the search, but thankfully there were no other terrorists hiding out on the aircraft and waiting to do us any harm, and at the end of the day I went home to my family.

CHAPTER SEVEN

The Police Firearms Situation in Northern Ireland

The arming of police officers in Northern Ireland has always been a very different scenario compared with county-wide police forces throughout the rest of the United Kingdom.

Between 1822 and 1922 Ireland was policed by the quasi-military Royal Irish Constabulary (RIC), which was supported by two paramilitary forces: the Auxiliaries and the Ulster Special Constabulary (USC). The Auxiliaries were founded in July 1920 by Major General Henry Hugh Tudor and were comprised of ex-British Army officers, most of whom had served during the First World War. Their main purpose was to carry out armed counter-insurgency operations against the Irish Republican Army, but it was disbanded in 1922 as a direct result of the Anglo-Irish Treaty.

The Ulster Special Constabulary, meanwhile, was formed in October 1920 and was a reserve special constabulary. All its members were armed and were generally called upon during times of emergencies. It remained operational until 31 March 1970, when it was disbanded.

There was also the group known as the Black and Tans, which for the most part was also comprised of former British Army soldiers.

They were police Constables used as reinforcements by the Royal Irish Constabulary and were recruited from January 1920 onwards, following a suggestion by the British unionist leader, Walter Long. Although still members of the Royal Irish Constabulary, the Black and Tans were specifically recruited in England and their name was derived from their mixed uniform of a dark RIC tunic and British Army khaki trousers. They were disbanded in 1922 at the same time as the RIC.

The Royal Ulster Constabulary (RUC) was formed on 1 June 1922, following the partition of Ireland. It was seen by many nationalists as a force put in place simply to enforce British rule. From the outset they were heavily armed because of the potential threat against them from Irish paramilitary groups who wanted a united Ireland. As well as side arms, they also routinely carried submachine guns and drove round in armoured Land Rovers. Even the police stations they worked out of were heavily fortified.

Due to the unique situation of policing in Northern Ireland, life for serving officers was a particularly dangerous one. A 1983 report written by Interpol showed that Northern Ireland was 'the most dangerous place in the world to be a police officer. The risk factor being twice as high as in El Salvador, the second most dangerous.'

It was on Tuesday, 10 August 1993 that the then Chief Constable of the RUC, Sir Hugh Annesley, announced that female officers serving in the RUC were to be armed from April 2004, although there were some women who were armed from October 2003. Where possible, these officers were restricted to driving duties and not sent out foot patrols.

The RUC was dissolved on 4 November 2001 as part of the Good Friday Agreement and replaced with the Police Service of Northern Ireland (PSNI). After the Metropolitan Police in London and Police Scotland, it is the third largest police force in the United Kingdom but remains the only one where all its officers are permanently armed on a day-to-day basis. Their officers can also call upon the use of water cannon vehicles capable of shooting high-velocity streams of water at either individuals or crowds of people. They can also use what are now referred to as attenuating energy projectiles, or what were more commonly referred to as rubber bullets.

In the 2005 book *The Thin Green Line: The History of the Royal Ulster Constabulary*, written by RUC Reservist Richard Doherty, during the existence of the RUC, 314 of its officers were killed and more than 9,000 were injured. Out of these, 302 were killed during what have since become known as The Troubles of 1969 and 1998. Figures also show that 277 of the officers who were killed during these times were murdered in attacks carried out by Irish republican organisations.

These statistics alone highlight just how dangerous life was for men and women of the RUC and more latterly the PSNI, regardless of whether they carried firearms or not. Sadly, the name change of the police service in the province appears to have come about more for political appeasement than the safety and wellbeing of the men and women who serve within its ranks, as their requirement to carry firearms as part of their general police duties has not changed.

CHAPTER EIGHT

Cheshire Constabulary - A Brief History of their Firearms Unit

Chris Clarke was a firearms officer with Cheshire Constabulary in the 1980s and 1990s. He began his time as a divisional AFO, which meant he worked out of his particular police station undergoing general police duties and was called upon to fulfil his role as a firearms officer only as and when he was required to do so. After that he then became a part-time member of the Firearms Support Unit (FSU), then later a full-time member. After several years fulfilling that particular role, he became a firearms instructor, training others to be able to undertake bodyguard and hostage rescue duties. He also became one of the unit's tactical advisors, as was usual for all instructors.

Changes within the force from a firearms perspective came about in the 1980s, when AFOs became a divisional responsibility and the weaponry available for use consisted of Smith & Wesson models 10 handguns, which used .38 special ammunition. Officers were typically issued with eighteen rounds, as and when they were deployed on a firearms operation. This came from the divisional armoury which was usually kept in a firearms safe located in the Superintendent's office. Officers could also be issued with

Remington 870 Wingmaster shotguns, if required, which fired 00 buck ammunition.

To qualify as a firearms officer, those concerned underwent a two-week course where they would undergo training both in the use of firearms and tactics. In the shooting aspect of the course, they only had to achieve an average of 70% to pass, hitting the target from different distances, in different positions. The tactical aspect of the course involved training in building containment and entries, as well as another aspect not always considered from a police firearms aspect: animal destruction.

To maintain their firearms authorisation, officers had to requalify every three months, alternating between shooting practice on the range and tactical days. With the introduction of the FSU in the early 1980s, the intention was that the AFOs would back up their better trained and more experienced counterparts as and when they were required to do so. Prior to this they would be the ones used in all firearm-related situations. When carrying out such work, officers simply wore their everyday uniform and were issued with a revolver, a holster and belt – in those days, officers were not even issued with body armour.

The force's FSU was formed in the early 1980s in response to an increased demand for the police use of firearms throughout Cheshire, although to begin with, it was not a full-time entity. The unit consisted of around thirty-five officers, including one full-time Inspector and three Sergeants who worked on the unit on a part-time basis. The rest were Constables who were also utilised on a part-time basis. They were deployed on a call out basis to begin with and would be sent to firearms incidents around the county when needed, where they would be met by a force mobile armoury which carried weapons, ammunition and all other relevant equipment they might need to carry out the task at hand. Their personal equipment had improved somewhat, with all firearms officers equipped with overalls, body armour, respirator, boots, gloves and a belt.

To be selected for the FSU, officers had to complete a basic AFO course then a further three-week FSU course. On the latter of the two courses, they had to achieve an 80% average shooting accuracy on the range. They also underwent training in the use of CS gas and respirators, advanced searches and rapid house entry tactics, vehicle stops, working with drugs, customs and terrorism units. The course also included instruction on close protection duties for VIPs visiting the county. Typically, the training for FSU officers was two days per month, which would include one day's shooting on the range with several different weapons, which included Smith & Wesson pistols, shotguns, Remington 'sniper rifles', and Ruger carbines. The second day consisted of practising differing tactics. During my time as a firearms officer, not every force undertook the same type of training. Although the very nature of the work meant the training had to be of a high standard, there was no uniformity across the country in the tactics used or the amount of specific shooting time officers were given. This was decided by each force. Times have now changed and no matter the police force, the firearms training is the same. This allows officers from one force to assist those from another force if required, knowing full well that the tactics used will be the same.

Selected FSU officers were also trained in the use of long-distance rifles, often referred to in the press as sniper rifles. All the different training, whether in weaponry or tactics, was carried out by qualified instructors, all of whom had attended national instructor courses, national bodyguard courses and national rifle courses, which were held within a number of force areas up and down the country, including the Metropolitan, Devon & Cornwall, Northumbria, Lancashire, West Mercia and Northern Ireland police forces.

In the early 1990s Cheshire Constabulary made the decision to place the FSU instructor team on a full-time basis. The unit at that time consisted of an Inspector, two Sergeants and ten Constables.

To maintain their status as instructors, the expected shooting accuracy with all weapons was 90%, which had to be achieved monthly. As policing throughout Cheshire became more structured, the weaponry used by the county's authorised firearms officers was updated to Glock 17 9-mm handguns, because they were seen to be an extremely reliable weapon as well as being cost effective. The force also invested in a number of Glock 19 pistols, which in essence were the same weapon, just for those officers with smaller hands.

A number of Heckler & Koch 5.56-mm assault rifles with scopes were also purchased, as were the Heckler & Koch MP5 9-mm semi-automatic carbines, which were for standard use up to and including about 100 metres. MP5 Ds were purchased for hostage scenarios, while several Heckler & Koch MSG90 rifles were purchased for use in sniper-type situations. The force also had the capability to use CS munitions in the form of either grenades or shotgun cartridges, as well as baton gun launched munitions. The force's armoury also provided access to stun grenades and smoke for use in hostage situations.

Cheshire Constabulary maintained a hostage rescue team of twenty-five officers who trained one day per month to hone and maintain their particular skillset, though in Chris's time, they were never called upon operationally.

CHAPTER NINE

Essex Police – A Brief History of Their Central Firearms Unit

Before the invention of the Force Support Unit in 1973, Essex Police already had a firearms capability which dated back to the mid-1960s: the Armed Besieged Criminals Squad (ABC Squad). In the late 1960s the ABC Squad became the newly formed Armed Emergency Team (AET) and in 1971, the AET became the Central Firearms Unit (CFU). Those who were part of the unit had both .38 Smith & Wesson pistols as well as shotguns at their disposal.

The following is an article that appeared in the October 1973 edition of the Essex Police newspaper, *The Law*:

> With the criminal use of firearms becoming more widespread each year, and with the extensive press coverage given to the recent cases in London, in which a total of three armed criminals were shot dead by Police officers in the course of their duty, *The Law* has considered it is now the time to let a little more light fall on to this subject as it applies to our force, to show the Central Firearms Unit in its true perspective and

to give a brief history of the unit, its present composition and its intended functions.

The forerunner of the Central Firearms Unit (CFU) was formed in the mid-1960s and named the Armed Besieged Criminals Squad (ABC Squad).

Under the watchful eye of Sergeant Basil Shoulders, gas masks were issued to the ten members of the squad and the rest of the afternoon was spent in checking their efficiency. The session ended with each member firing one CS practice cartridge from a converted 37-mm Verey Light pistol.

With Force Firearms Training still in its infancy, the squad was intended as a 'back-up' unit to re-enforce armed divisional officers in a siege situation.

The year 1968 saw eight officers from this force attending a Firearms Instructors Course and the beginning of realistic firearms training before the following year.

The old ABC Squad came under the microscope, its short comings were recognised, and it was reorganised, enlarged, updated and equipped with .38 pistols .303 rifles and, under the command of Inspector John Page, was renamed the Armed Emergency Team (AET).

The CFU kept its strength to ten officers, based at the headquarters in Chelmsford, under the watchful eye of Inspector Page, who had previously served at Witham police station. Two of the early members of the CFU were Gus Bowers and Mick Branham. As far as can be ascertained, the officers on the unit received no specific firearms training at that time.

When called upon to attend a firearms-related incident, the officers would first have to draw their weapons and ammunition from a locked cupboard in the information room.

By 1979, Gus Bowers had become the force armourer for Essex Police.

CHAPTER TEN

Leicestershire Police – A Brief History of Their Firearms Unit

The Lambourne Road Siege in Leicester, which took place on 1 September 1975, began as a domestic incident when a Bulgarian-born individual named Sabi Nikoloff, 50, turned up at 25 Lambourne Road, the home of his ex-wife, the Swiss-born Betty Nikoloff, armed with a shotgun, before barricading himself inside. According to Betty, Nikoloff was a bit of a Jekyll and Hyde character, who would be nice and polite when they were in the company of friends, but once they were at home, he would beat her and their sons Nikolai and Ivan, as well as their daughter Angela. The only one to escape his wrath was the youngest son, Bruno. The continuous violence for Betty became so bad that during their marriage, she attempted suicide on three occasions.

By 1972, and after being married to Nikoloff for seventeen years, Betty had finally had enough and obtained a separation order from him, which gave her the house, custody of the children and forced Nikoloff to move out of the matrimonial home. He was not a happy man. Once the divorce became absolute in 1974, the court ordered that he would also have to pay Betty maintenance, which he refused to do, and which eventually saw him sent to prison for a period of six weeks.

It is unclear as to how Nikoloff came to be in possession of a double-barrelled shotgun and dozens of cartridges, not to mention the cans of petrol and oil. When he arrived at 25 Lambourne Road, Betty and two of her neighbours were outside the house, chatting. During the siege, one of the neighbours, Enid Cabaniuk, who had bravely given evidence against Nikoloff during his divorce from Betty, was shot dead in the street. Betty ran into her home and upstairs to her younger son, Bruno, while her other children ran from the house, fearing for their lives. Meanwhile, Nikoloff set fire to the house at the bottom of the stairs, so as to stop anybody else who might have entered from getting to the first floor.

Police were called and an unarmed male Sergeant and a female Constable were sent to investigate. Outside the house, a shot was fired and the Sergeant, Brian 'Geordie' Dawson, fell dead. His female colleague, Margaret Dayman, was also fired upon and hit. She survived but sustained serious injuries.

An off-duty police officer who lived in the road, Constable Don Acton, shielded his wounded police colleague and gave her first aid as best he could, and in doing so putting his own life at risk. He would later be awarded the George Medal for his brave and selfless actions that day. He was also famously photographed in tears at the funeral of his friend and colleague, Sergeant Dawson. An ambulance arrived in Lambourne Road and as it reversed with the back door open in an attempt to recover the wounded police officer, as well as the bodies of Sergeant Dawson and Mrs Cabaniuk, the driver, Terry Wilkinson, was shot after Nikoloff fired at the vehicle from the house, with the bullets shattering the fibreglass door. Other police officers arrived and tried to form a cordon around the house. Nikoloff continued to fire more shots, one of which grazed the side of an officer's head. Despite threatening to kill Betty, Nikoloff allowed both her and Bruno to escape down a ladder. After the siege had been underway for an hour and twenty minutes, the flames eventually became too much for Nikoloff and he jumped from the bedroom window. As he landed, he dropped his shotgun, which discharged upon hitting the floor, hitting the already wounded female Constable for a second time.

Nikoloff was detained at the scene in his front garden and appeared briefly at Leicester City Magistrates' Court on 3 and 12 September, when he was charged with three counts of murder for Sergeant Brian Dawson (42), ambulanceman Terence Williamson (33), and Mrs Enid Casinuick (48). He was initially remanded for eight days followed by a further seven days on his second appearance. Nikoloff was also charged with the attempted murder of WPC Margaret Dayman. He was also charged with setting fire to 25 Lambourne Road with the intent to endanger the lives of his wife and youngest son. On 10 February 1976, Nikoloff was sentenced to life imprisonment at Leicester Crown Court after he was found guilty of the three murders.

As a result of the Lambourne Road incident, and after a subsequent force inquiry, it was decided to form a designated team of firearms officers to deal with such incidents, and the Leicestershire Constabulary Tactical Firearms Unit came into existence in 1976. Back then, the constabulary had shotguns as well as .38 Smith & Wesson handguns that were stored safely in several police stations around the force area.

The newly formed unit consisted of twenty-four officers, who were deemed to be better shots than their fellow firearms officers, and who showed more of an aptitude for the tactical side of things. One of those original twenty-four officers was Constable Clive Dawkes, who along with his colleagues was on call on a week on and a week off basis, whilst still carrying out their normal police duties. They were given pagers for callouts and trained one day a week (always a Tuesday) to perfect and hone their skills in dealing with all firearms incidents within the force's area.

According to Sergeant Dawkes:

As always there were some who didn't want firearms to be deployed and would do whatever they could to try and resolve the matter in other ways, which was potentially an extremely dangerous strategy to say the least. We got the message across over time and gained the confidence of most senior officers in the way we dealt with all incidents.

We did some training with the Special Air Service (SAS) and gained knowledge and insight of how best it was to resolve firearms-related incidents. We also put in place regional training with neighbouring forces for when we crossed Force borders when incidents were on the move.

I became a firearms instructor in 1979 and I am proud to say that it was a position I remained in until my retirement in 1993, due to hearing loss because of the number of rounds I had heard fired in training. Thankfully, because of how good our training was, we never fired, or needed to fire, a shot in anger during my time as a firearms officer with Leicestershire Police.

Another response to deal with firearms incidents was to come later in the early 1990s, with the introduction of two Armed Response Vehicles (ARVs). Each were double crewed, and covered the entire 24-hour period, with the weapons stored in a secure cabinet in the rear of the vehicle. The idea was for the ARV to attend the scene of a firearms incident and set up and hold an initial cordon, until the TFU were requested and had arrived.

CHAPTER ELEVEN

West Midlands Police – A Brief History of Their Firearms Unit

Birmingham Borough Police, one of the forerunners of today's West Midlands Police, has a history which dates back to 1839. All those years ago, however, the only weapons the police were issued with were cutlasses and not firearms. In America, Samuel Colt did not begin manufacturing his revolvers until 1836, and Horace Smith and Daniel B. Wesson, better known as Smith & Wesson, only started manufacturing their pistols in 1857. Repeater-type rifles had been about in different guises for nearly 200 years in the early 1830s, but they were not used by the newly formed police forces throughout Britain.

Similar to the use of firearms within police forces today, there was strict control concerning the issue and use of cutlasses within the Birmingham Borough Police. In December 1841, a contingent of more than 150 Constables, Sergeants and senior officers, led Mr Burgess, the Chief Commissioner of Birmingham Borough Police, went to Bilston to help assist the local police, after the magistrates there had applied to the authorities in Birmingham after concerns that a planned number of meetings in the town, organised by the leaders of the local Chartist movement, might lead to violent clashes over the course of the festive period. To ensure matters did not get totally out of hand, the Constables, who were all in possession of cutlasses, were told that they were 'on no account to use them' unless they were expressly told to do so by the magistrates in Bilston.

Possibly one of the first cases of a police officer being involved in the act of a 'negligent discharge' of a firearm occurred in Birmingham in 1868. An article in the *Birmingham Journal* dated Saturday, 28 March, reported how Superintendent Wilcox, Inspector Timmins and Constable Joseph Gordon, all members of the Birmingham Borough Police, were amusing themselves by practising with their revolvers at Alcester Street police station. After several shots had been fired, Superintendent Wilcox, thinking that all the cartridges had been discharged from his revolver, attempted to extract the spent cartridges. It turned out, however, that a loaded cartridge remained, and in attempting to remove it, he caused it to explode. Constable Gordon, who was standing near Wilcox and taking the spent cartridges from his own revolver, was hit in the face when the ball from Wilcox's weapon entered via his cheek and fractured his jaw, but only after it had ricocheted a number of times round the rear yard. Mr Thomas, a local surgeon who lived near the police station, was called immediately, but despite his best attempts was unable to locate the ball. Constable Gordon was then taken to Birmingham's Queen's Hospital, where he was seen by a Dr Jolly, who was also unable to extract the ball.

On Saturday, 14 November 1885, a letter dated Tuesday, 3 November 1885 appeared in *The Police Guardian* publication. The letter had been sent in by the Chief of Police, Coventry, Mr John Norris, who had put pen to paper in the immediate aftermath of the murder of a police constable in Cumberland.

It read as follows:

Dear Sir,

The Netherby Hall mournful tragedy, together with numerous other murderous attacks upon police officers by armed burglars at nighttime will convince rational and well-disposed persons that the time has arrived that the constable on night duty should be furnished with a proper weapon of defence and trained to the use of such; otherwise, proper protection to property and life will cease. Police authorities cannot demand a solitary officer at a lonely spot, in the dead of night, to face or challenge a gang of wilful desperadoes without they first provide him with proper means of defence. The fact of it's becoming known that the police carried a weapon would act as a deterrent to those cowardly wretches who prowl about for dishonest purposes. The courage, conduct and faithful services of the police have been admitted and praised in the House of Commons over and over again, and yet little or nothing has been done for their protection or benefit by this honoured assembly. It is too bad to allow good men to be murdered and otherwise ill-used, without any effort being made to furnish the means for their better personal safety and benefit.

With best wishes, for those brave men now suffering in Cumberland and much sympathy with the distressed relatives of the murdered officer.

I am dear Sir,
Yours truly

John Norris
Chief of Police, Coventry

This letter shows that the debate concerning whether or not police officers should carry firearms is not a recent one, but it is remarkable to think of what was expected of police officers, especially whilst working on their own during the dark of night, in a time before police vehicles or radios. Many years later, during the First World War, Birmingham City Police officers were issued with firearms. With concerns over the presence of German spies, this was felt particularly relevant when officers were on night patrols.

When a police officer is involved a shooting incident, it is not only the officer who it effects, but their family as well. On Saturday, 22 July 1972, Anna Marie Guthrie became the youngest ever police widow after her husband, 21-year-old Police Constable Peter Charles Guthrie, a Constable with the Warwickshire and Coventry Police, was shot whilst investigating a burglary at a sports shop in Far Gosford Street, Coventry. Anna Marie was just 17 years of age and had only been married for six weeks when her husband was killed. Unbeknown to PC Guthrie, the perpetrator, Charles Jeffs, was still on the premises after the burglary had been reported and had in his possession a shotgun, which he had been intending to steal from the shop. Jeffs fired the weapon, hitting PC Guthrie in the chest and thigh and leaving him with fatal injuries.

Police Sergeant Gordon Meredith arrived at the premises soon after PC Guthrie, by which time the latter had already been shot. As he entered the shop, PS Meredith saw Jeffs trying to climb out of a rear window and lunged at him, grabbing hold of the shotgun in the process. A struggle ensued and the gun went off, resulting in PS Meredith being shot in the thigh. He still held onto the weapon, causing Jeffs to let go of it and escape. Other officers were soon in attendance and gave chase before catching and arresting him, even though he had a military-style bayonet in his possession at the time.

PC Guthrie was posthumously awarded the Queen's Police Medal for Gallantry, whilst PS Meredith was awarded the George Medal for his bravery.

Jeffs' trial began on Tuesday, 7 November 1972, where he was charged with the murder of PC Guthrie and the attempted murder of PS Meredith: allegations to which he pleaded not guilty, claiming that he did not intentionally shoot either officer, and that whilst he was struggling with PS Meredith, he did not recall even having his finger on the trigger of the shotgun. The trial concluded the following day when the jury found Jeffs guilty on both counts. The judge, Mr Justice Ashworth, sentenced him to life imprisonment, with a recommendation that he serve at least twenty years before he could be considered for parole.

After sentencing, Mr Justice Ashworth said the following about PC Guthrie and PS Meredith:

PC Guthrie was killed performing his duty with quite exemplary courage. Sergeant Meredith too, behaved with exemplary courage.

One has only got to think of the scene in Far Gosford Street. He arrives and hears a shot. He must have guessed that one of his younger officers had been wounded and maybe killed. Then he sees the terrible young man emerging from the window with a gun. It was a moment which would have taxed the courage of many men. It did not daunt Sergeant Meredith for a moment.

I think his performance of grabbing the gun when it could have gone off at any time, and his presence of mind in diverting the barrel away from his heart, showed courage of a very high order.

Once again, this is a fine example of the bravery of police officers who had no means of defending themselves. Even if PC Guthrie had been in possession of a firearm, it is unlikely that he would have had it drawn, because as far as he was concerned, he was simply attending a burglary. As for PS Meredith, if he had been armed, he could have used the weapon to defend himself and would have more than likely prevented himself from being shot, as he would not have needed to struggle with Jeffs.

The robbery described above is another example of just how dangerous society was becoming in the early 1970s, especially for police officers. It was as if the abolition of the death penalty for murder had encouraged some elements of the criminal fraternity to use firearms when carrying out their crimes, knowing full well that even if they were caught, they would not face the hangman's noose.

The West Midlands Constabulary had a relatively short life span, only being in existence for eight years between 1 April 1966 and 31 March 1974, when it became the West Midlands Police. It had originally come into being as a direct result of the Police Act 1964. In 1974 it amalgamated with the Birmingham City Police, parts of Staffordshire County and Stoke-on-Trent Constabulary, Warwickshire and Coventry Constabulary and West Mercia Constabulary, following the Local Government Act 1972.

Soon after the West Midlands Police was formed, a decision was taken that their response to firearms, like a number of other forces across the country, would become a more structured one, although there had been a more considered approach towards police use of firearms since October 1970, when it had still been the West Midlands Constabulary. To this end it was decided to have two levels of firearms capability. The first was an elite unit consisting of twenty officers, including four firearms instructors, who would carry out all pre-planned firearms operations across the West Midlands policing area. In addition to this unit, Authorised Firearms Officers (AFOs) would be based across the different policing districts. This strategy allowed for the divisional AFOs to initially attend and contain a firearms-related incident to give the force's full-time unit, who internally were referred to as the Top Squad (later changed to Special Squad), time to get to the location and deal with the situation.

It was around the same time that female officers first became AFOs, not just in the West Midlands Police, but in forces across the country. This highlighted a problem which had not even been previously considered. For some of the more petite women, the grips on handguns such as the Smith & Wesson were simply too big, which made it difficult for them to be able to grip the weapon properly. This was an issue which was easily rectified by putting smaller grips on the guns, but what was not so easy to rectify, however, was the size of weapons such as shotguns, which had the added problem for smaller female officers of a very powerful recoil. To fire a shotgun, the butt of it has to be held tightly into the top of the shoulder, and with most female officers being smaller and less physically stronger than their male counterparts, this posed a potential problem.

The first man in charge of the newly formed West Midlands Police firearms unit was Chief Inspector John Gash. Once a month he and his select band of firearms officers would meet at an underground firearms range in Walsall to undergo shooting practice and training exercises, to ensure that all the officers maintained the required standard of shooting to be able to remain a member of the unit. Those on the unit were selected 'due to their cool temperament, their ability to keep calm under pressure, and to have a sound judgement'.

It was clear that Chief Inspector Gash was proud of the men he served with: 'We are continually training men to make them as efficient as we possibly can with weapons, although we hope they will never be used.' He also added: 'It would be a sad day for the police of this country if violence ever reached a point where every officer had to be armed.'

In 1980, an incident occurred in the West Midlands that highlighted the difficult situations police officers called upon to take part in firearms operations, face on a daily basis. On Friday,

11 July 1980, Gail Kinchin, a pregnant 16-year-old girl, died in the intensive care unit at the East Birmingham Hospital, having been shot four times by members of the West Midlands Police Firearms Operations Unit (FOU) at just after 2am on 12 June. She had initially been admitted to Birmingham's Selly Oak Hospital where she had undergone emergency surgery. It was during the surgery that her unborn baby was pronounced dead.

Kinchin had been shot after armed police had entered a maisonette in Rubery, Birmingham, where she was being held hostage by ex-paratrooper David Pagett, the father of her unborn child. The incident had begun when Pagett, armed with a shotgun, had first burst into to the house of Kinchin's stepfather and mother, in the Kings Heath area of Birmingham, demanding to see her, even though she was staying with friends in Rubery at the time.

The incident ended with Pagett holding Kinchin hostage at the maisonette in Rubery. In an attempt to escape, Pagett used Kinchin as a human shield whilst at the same time firing his 12-bore shotgun at the armed police officers trying to arrest him. The shotgun blast missed the officers, but when they returned fire, their shots missed Pagett and four rounds fired by two police officers struck Kinchin, who had been trying to break free from Pagett. Having been shot, Kinchin fell backwards on to him, knocking him to the floor and causing him to drop the shotgun, which then went off. The shot rebounded off the concrete floor, injuring him in the process.

When the matter went to court in March 1981, Pagett conducted his own defence. After he had called ten witnesses to give evidence on his behalf, he was informed by the judge that none of the witnesses he had called had added anything to what the jury had heard from the prosecution witnesses. Pagett then informed the judge that he intended to call about thirty-five other witnesses, only to be told that he ought to be careful that these new witnesses should add something to the case.

At the end of the trial, Pagett was found guilty of Miss Kinchin's manslaughter, the attempted murder of the two police firearms officers who opened fire, Miss Kinchin's stepfather, and the kidnapping of her mother. He was sentenced to twelve years' imprisonment. Despite attempts by Pagett's legal representatives to have the two police marksmen charged with Kinchin's murder, it was decided that the officers who fired the fatal shots would not be prosecuted.

Pagett was released in 1988, having served just seven years, but was jailed again the following year for the rape of a prostitute.

On 24 August 1985, the difficulties which potentially faced every firearms officer up and down the country were once again horrifically highlighted, when members of the West Midlands Tactical Firearms Unit, who were part-time firearms officers, meaning that their day-to-day policing role involved other duties and that they carried out firearms operations as and when they were needed to do so, carried out a raid on a house near Kings Norton in Birmingham. They were looking for a man by the name of John Shorthouse, who was suspected of having carried out an armed robbery in Wales, which led them to believe that Shorthouse might be in possession of a pump-action shotgun. During the subsequent raid on the premises in Kings Norton, one of the firearms officers, armed with a Smith & Wesson .38 revolver with no safety catch, was conducting a search of one of the bedrooms. As he looked under the bed, he placed the hand holding his revolver on the mattress to pull himself up, but when he did, the gun went off, discharging a round into the bed. Unfortunately for the officer concerned, hidden under the blankets was John Shorthouse's 5-year-old son, also named John. The round struck him in the chest and killed him. The officer was suspended from duty and after an investigation into the tragic and accidental shooting, was subsequently charged with manslaughter and put before the courts to stand trial. He was found not guilty and returned to duty.

Not only was this a tragedy for the family of the young boy, but it also highlighted the difficulties faced by police officers who volunteered to carry firearms for operation police purposes. In this particular case, an officer had not intentionally discharged his firearm, fearing for his life, that of a fellow officer, or a member of the public. It was simply a tragic accident. Despite this, the officer concerned not only faced losing his job, but if he had been found guilty as charged, he also faced the frightening prospect of being sent to prison for a number of years.

The officer who shot John Shorthouse was a beat officer, who the day before the shooting had been carrying out foot patrol duties on the streets of Coventry. In the immediate aftermath of the shooting, this led to much debate as to how the West Midlands Police dealt with and approached their response to firearms incidents. The then Chief Constable, Geoffrey Dear, took the decision to form a full-time firearms unit, which in essence reduced the number of officers authorised to carry firearms, whilst at the same time improved the training and equipment that the officers who were members of the unit used.

The tactical side of the training now focused heavily on siege situations and search techniques in houses and flats: scenarios and locations officers were more than likely to find themselves having to operate in on a regular basis. To keep the officers at their peak, they alternated their duties between training, carrying out firearms operations, or patrolling Birmingham airport.

The decision by Chief Constable Dear to create a full-time firearms unit was not met with universal approval. Members of his very own police authority had grave concerns:

> My fear is that we are moving towards making the police a paramilitary force, I am against creating elitism. It is dangerous because you create a special person and that

is even more dangerous in the police force. Within a few weeks of the life of the new police authority we were making decisions about plastic bullets, and we have talk now from Sir Kenneth Newman the Metropolitan Police Commissioner of armoured vehicles. Where is it going to stop?

Despite these misgivings the West Midlands FOU was up and running by 1987, by which time those forces who had not already taken a similar approach to the firearms aspect of policing were instructed by the then Home Secretary Douglas Hurd, that they must take a similar approach.

Audux in Periculis, meaning bold in danger, was the name chosen as the motto of the unit and just happened to be the family motto of one of its first officers.

Constables Julie McAloon and Jaine Simner became the first female officers to become members of the FOU in 1990.

On 19 December 1988, Police Constable Gavin Carlton was shot dead after following a suspect vehicle containing two men believed to be responsible for carrying out an armed robbery at the Midland Bank in Tile Hill, Coventry. PC Carlton was single crewed and unarmed and had been responding to an alarm at the bank. Just as he arrived at the scene, he saw a car making off and after following it for a short distance, the vehicle stopped suddenly, and shots were fired towards PC Carlton, causing his car to swerve and the front of it to hit a bollard. One of the suspects got out of their vehicle walked up to PC Carlton, who was still sat in his vehicle, and shot him at point-blank range, killing him.

The two suspects, Nicholas Hill and David Fisher, then fled the scene. Unarmed Detectives Constable Len Jakeman and Trevor Ginn, who were actually on their way to court, heard a call in relation to the shooting over their police radio and decided to respond. They spotted the suspect vehicle soon afterwards in Torrington Avenue and sped after it. Not long after, the two suspects abandoned their vehicle and made off into some flats. The two detectives followed them on foot and at one stage were shot at. The two suspects kept on running until they got into another vehicle parked on the other side of the flats. DC Ginn managed to get back to their car, picked up DC Jakeman enroute, and gave chase. Without any concern for their own wellbeing, DC Ginn decided to crash their car into that of the suspect's, which stopped it in its tracks. If that was not brave enough, the two officers leapt out of their vehicle and approached the suspects, despite knowing they had already shot one of their colleagues and had had fired at them earlier on. A struggle ensued in which the two suspects got out of their vehicle. At one stage one of them pointed a shotgun at the head of DC Jakeman before lowering it to his stomach and pulling the trigger. The two suspects again made off and despite the danger, DC Ginn once again chased after them, despite the fact that they continued firing their shotgun.

The two men were eventually traced to an empty house in Stoneleigh Avenue, Earlsdon. West Midlands FOU were requested to attend the location, and twenty members of the unit arrived in under thirty minutes. Attempts were made to make both men realise that further resistance was futile and that their only realistic option was to surrender. This eventually resulted in Nicholas Hill surrendering and walking out with his hands in the air. Shortly after he had left the building, a shot rang out. When the police entered, they saw David Fisher slumped in a chair: he had shot himself in the head.

Both DCs Ginn and Jakeman were awarded the George Medal for their extremely brave actions on that fateful day. DC Jakeman spent twenty months recovering from his injuries and did not return to full duties until August 1990, before retiring in 1993.

Whilst being interviewed by police, Hill told officers that one of the reasons they chose the Midland Bank in Coventry was because they knew that West Midlands Police had no Armed Response capability, which meant they had worked out it would be at least half an hour after they had committed their robbery before armed police officers would even arrive on the scene.

As a direct result of that information, and within only a matter of months, the Chief Constable of the West Midlands Police, Geoffrey Dear, brought in the force's first Armed Response Vehicle (ARV), which was up and running by March 1989. By 1995, the number of ARVs had increased to three.

CHAPTER TWELVE

Avon & Somerset, Gloucestershire, and Wiltshire's Tri-Force Specialist Operations Unit

In December 2012, Avon & Somerset, Gloucestershire, and Wiltshire police forces set up the Tri-Force Specialist Operations Unit, which included road policing, firearms and the dog section. Its purpose was to form a centrally managed, intelligence-led, specialist policing unit, intended for use anywhere across the three force areas. It was felt there was a need for such a collaboration in the area following an increase in acts of terrorism and domestic extremism across the country, and that it would provide 'more efficiency by sharing resources' for all three forces. Over the life of the 'alliance' several reviews made recommendations to improve the effectiveness of the partnership, while also highlighting such issues as the different briefing systems, policies and IT. On Tuesday, 20 November 2021, it was announced by Avon & Somerset Constabulary's Chief Constable Sarah Crew, and Police and Crime Commissioner (PCC) Mark Shelford, that for the previous seven months all three partners had been working to revise the terms of their collaboration, as recommended by the independent reviews, but that sadly, they had been unable to reach an agreement on the finite details. They went on to say that:

> Unfortunately, we have not been able to reconcile the need highlighted by the reports to improve the effectiveness of the collaboration with our partners' requirements to retain control staff in their areas, therefore leaving us with no option but to withdraw from the Tri-force Specialist Operations collaboration. Working together with our neighbouring forces and with other partners makes absolute common sense. It shares our expertise, training and costs, however it has got to work in the interests of all parties, for our staff and residents and where it is efficient and effective to do so.

The arrangement that all three forces had in place was due to expire on 19 April 2019, so rather than bring it to an end before that date, all parties kept the partnership going until then. It was initially hoped that the armed response aspect of the agreement could be kept alive, but the proposal on this aspect was that for a new structure to work effectively, direction and control of armed response policing in Wiltshire should be passed to the Chief Constable of Avon & Somerset. This was something that the police in Wiltshire were understandably not able to accept, with Wiltshire's PCC saying that he was unable to accept the proposal, 'as it ran counter to his strong belief in local accountability'. He later added that he believed, 'If a firearms incident occurs in Wiltshire, it is right and proper that the Chief Constable of Wiltshire should be accountable to me; just as I am accountable to the people of Wiltshire and Swindon.' It seemed to be a fair response.

The centralised unit was disbanded on 19 April 2019, having been in existence for nearly six years, after the former of the three forces pulled out of the agreement. With Gloucestershire and Wiltshire being unable to come to an agreement to continue as a bi-force unit, all three forces went their separate ways.

Despite the breakup, all three forces continued to conduct their firearms training at the Black Rock Training Centre in Portishead, Somerset. The opening of the centre, which had originally been due to open in 2014, was delayed due to a fire caused by an arson attack in August 2013. It was eventually opened by Prime Minister Theresa May in December 2015, and catered for both firearms and public order training, with the three forces collaborating to form a reginal firearms unit, which consisted of men and women from all three forces. Besides the logistical advantages, the collaboration also saw a collective saving of £3.5 million.

The state-of-the-art facility included an area where officers could hone their skills in the art of abseiling. There are also several firearms ranges, as well as different types of life-like interactive target systems.

In principle, the tri-force collaboration was a forward-thinking idea, but while the driving force behind the idea appears to have been a financial one, the firearms aspect of it was always going to be difficult to sustain due to the potential for having to hand over responsibility and control of a firearms operation to another force, which might then end up in a fatal shooting. This would then pose the problem of which force would need to refer themselves to the Independent Police Complaints Commission (IPCC): the force area where the shooting took place, or the one who had overall command of the operation? After all, these might not be one and the same.

CHAPTER THIRTEEN

Aidrian 'Aide' Smart: Ex-Firearms Instructor, Essex Police

Aidrian Smart, known to his family, friends and ex-colleagues as Aide, had a long involvement with firearms in the Essex Police, as a member of the Tactical Firearms Group and later as an instructor. As well as working with operationally, he was also one of my instructors on my own basic firearms course.

Aidrian began his time with Essex Police back in November 1972, just after his twenty-first birthday, initially being posted to what was then the Grays policing division. Having spent three years learning his craft as a uniformed bobby on the beat, he decided he would like a change of scenery and to be closer to his family, and so he found himself transferred to the Colchester division in 1975.

In 1977 he saw an internal advert looking for volunteers interested in becoming a divisional firearms officer, which meant they would remain working on division, but be called upon from time to time to take part in firearms operations throughout the Colchester policing area. Those officers interested in becoming an Authorised Firearms Officer had to attend a one-day assessment at police headquarters, Chelmsford. If the officers were successful on their assessment, they would then be given a one-week basic firearms training course.

Having given it some thought, it sounded both interesting and exciting to young Aidrian, so he decided to apply. He passed both the one-day assessment and the subsequent one-week's basic firearms course, which meant that he now possessed a firearms permit authorising him to carry firearms for police purposes.

The one-day assessment consisted of several scenarios that tested an officer's basic shooting ability, temperament, presentation, questioning and justification in the use of firearms in stressful situations. The assessment was run by the firearms instructors of the time, one of whom was the late Brian 'Bill' Bishop, who was shot dead on a firearms operation in Frinton, Essex in 1984 (see Chapter Nineteen). Aidrian would later go onto work with Brian when they were both members of Essex Police's Tactical Firearms Group (TFG). Besides being colleagues, they also went onto become good friends.

Later that year, Aidrian underwent his basic firearms course, which lasted for just one week. An interesting point worth mentioning here is that by the time I took my basic firearms course eleven years later, the same course had been increased to five weeks.

Aidrian's basic course saw him pit his wits and his desire to qualify as a firearms officer against eleven other students, who all had similar designs. They were of different ages and backgrounds, had a variation of policing skills and lengths of service, and were from all different parts of the county.

The course began with the students being introduced to a .38 Smith & Wesson 4-inch revolver. The weapon was a very straight forward piece of equipment to use. There was nothing complicated about it at all. It was simply a case of point, aim, squeeze the trigger and fire. The students needed to be proficient in its use, however, because at the end of the week they had to pass a live firing test, which consisted of shooting from distances of 5, 7, 10, 15, 20 and 25 metres, in either the prone position, kneeling or standing. The shooting part of the course was only part of what decided if a student ultimately passed or failed. Besides discovering whether their shooting abilities were good enough, there was also an equal emphasis placed on an individual's tactical abilities in scenarios set by the instructors. These included how to search buildings safely, vehicle tactics, open-country searches and personal confrontation-type scenarios, including verbal challenges and justification of a student's individual actions, all of which were designed to place them in stressful situations. After all, on a live firearms operation, an officer would ultimately have to be able to keep calm, digest information quickly, respond appropriately and not allow themselves to be overwhelmed by the stress of the situation that confronted them.

By the end of the course, not everybody was successful and for those who failed, the decision was based on any number of factors. Aidrian was one of the students who passed and became a divisional AFO. Although he remained stationed at Colchester, his duties now included having to undergo firearms training once a month, which would alternate between shooting practice and tactical searches.

Two years later Aidrian was still a divisional AFO, although by then he was stationed at Braintree police station, where he had been posted due to shortages of area car drivers. In 1979 he answered an internal advert requesting volunteers to join the county's Force Support Unit (FSU), which by then had only been in existence for six years. It dealt with all kinds of different incidents in support of the numerous policing divisions dotted around the county. This included firearms incidents, public disorder incidents, crowd control at football matches, house-to-house enquiries, mobile crime patrols, surveillance and searches, to name but a few. Aidrian was successful in his application, which would have been greatly assisted by the fact that he already had a firearms permit.

At that time the FSU had just three sections, each of which consisted of a Sergeant and ten Constables. These were all overseen by an Inspector, and above him were a command team of more senior officers. Two of the sections had advanced training in the use of firearms, weapons and tactics. The Tactical Firearms Group (TFG), along with the firearms instructors, made up an additional section. This consisted of an Inspector, Sergeant and six Constables. All the firearms instructors were given the temporary rank of acting Sergeant. The third and fourth sections (Aidrian had been allocated to the latter), consisted of officers who had successfully completed a basic firearms course and who would support the TFG when and if needed to do so. At the time, not all the officers who were in the third and fourth sections were firearms trained, but most were. In time, this changed so that everybody on the FSU, or applying to join it, had to be a qualified firearms officer.

Soon after joining the FSU, it was decided that a third section of officers with advanced training was needed because of a marked increase in the number of firearms operations the FSU was being asked to undertake. An advanced tactical course was put together by the force's firearms instructors, and those officers who were members of either sections three or four, who were already in possession of a firearms permit, were selected to undertake it. Aidrian was not only one of those selected to be on the course, but one of those who passed.

There were now sufficient officers to make up a third TFG section, all of whom were trained and qualified in the use of a .38 revolver, shotgun and .223 rifle. In addition to this a small number of officers were trained as snipers, although for political reasons, these officers were referred to as riflemen.

Each section of the FSU, regardless of whether they were a TFG section or non-TFG, all had to undergo monthly training, which was rotated between shooting and tactics, with officers having to re-qualify on all weapons every three months. The shooting requirements were particularly stringent, especially where qualification shoots were concerned. Anybody who did not reach the required standard would lose their firearms permit, which would temporarily prevent them from taking part in firearms operations. The officer concerned would then have to undergo what was referred to as refresher training, in an effort to identify and resolve an individual's particular shooting problems.

As previously discussed, the make-up of a section on most firearms operations consisted of a Raid Team made up of Raid 1 (R1) and Raid 2 (R2) and then Support 1 (S1), down to how ever many officers were required for each job. Those officers who made up the positions of the R1 and R2 did so because they had been identified by the training staff as having the required ability to lead the team during a live operation. To an extent, this was the same for the individual who undertook the role of the S1, who was the immediate supporting team member for the Raid Team, as well as being the link between them and the rest of the deployed team.

Most sections would have their designated Raid Team and S1, but ultimately it was down to the Tactical Firearms Commander (TFC), who in most cases would be the section Sergeant, but not always, to decide who the R1 was going to be for any given operation. It would then be down to the R1 to decide who they wanted as their R2. Both officers would have been experienced in their individual roles and would have worked with the other on a regular basis, both operationally and in training. Most sections would also have members who had shown potential to become an R1 or R2, and from time to time they would also be given the opportunity to lead the team.

At an early stage of his training, Aidrian was identified as having the potential to become member of the Raid Team, and after undertaking the role in training and on live operations, he became a fully fledged member.

After this, it was not too long before Aidrian was asked if he would like to become an instructor. As far as he was concerned, it was simply too good an opportunity to refuse. When he initially took up the role it was under the tutelage of the full-time instructors, who provided him with the necessary guidance and direction.

In 1981 he was sent to Devon & Cornwall Police, who at the time were one of only four forces in the country qualified to provide such instruction, to undergo a National Firearms Instructors course. The course was intense, as would be expected, and lasted for six weeks. The shooting aspect worked towards a qualification shoot on four different weapons. These were the .38 Smith & Wesson, 2- and 4-inch barrelled versions, the 9-mm Browning handgun, as well as a pump-action shotgun. The handgun aspect was particularly hard going, as all students had to be able to shoot on timed turning targets from different distances up to and including 25 metres, some using their weaker hand. These were done from several different positions, including standing, kneeling, and prone from behind a barrier.

The shotgun qualification included moving tactically from 100 metres, whilst engaging timed turning targets from various distances using what is known as slug ammunition, or one solid piece of lead.

Aidrian and his fellow students had been informed at the start of the course that the final qualification shoot would be on the day before the last day of the course and that failure on any of the four weapons, no matter how well the rest of the course had gone, would be an overall course failure. No pressure. The required pass percentage was 85% on each of the weapons.

The rest of the course was made up of developing the student's ability to teach up-and-coming firearms officers when they returned to their individual forces. This was done in a classroom environment as well as on a shooting range, which included safety procedures and the delivery of all aspects of the tactical use of the police use of firearms, as written down by the Home Office.

Preparation of lectures was given high importance. The students were given diverse subjects to research and were asked to give a lecture to the rest of the students and the instructors. This included hand-drawn overheads. All the lectures had to be precisely timed down to the last minute and had to be prepared in the students' own time in the evenings, as well as over the course of the weekend, where family time was precious, especially for those who had to travel long distances to get home.

At the end of the six weeks, Aidrian successfully passed all aspects of the course and returned to Essex as a qualified instructor. Within Essex Police, each of the instructors was given primary responsibility for training the various firearms user groups within the force, and a secondary role to a fellow instructors' group. Aidrian was given the task of training the different sections of the Tactical Firearms Group, with a secondary role of training Special Branch officers in the required skills of what was known as Close Protection. Special Branch were instructed in close quarter weapon range work and their training included producing a weapon from a hip or shoulder holster at speed and engaging quick turning targets. Another of their training aspects focused on foot and vehicle formations, as well as tactics specifically designed around VIP protection.

Despite having trained Special Branch officers in both shooting and tactics for a number of years, it was decided by the Home Office in about 1988 that there was a need for those instructors involved in training Special Branch officers to undergo and pass a National Close Protection Course in techniques as described in the *Manual of Guidance on Police Use of Firearms.* Aidrian was sent on this course, which took place at West Yorkshire Police Headquarters, Wakefield. The course lasted for three weeks and involved preparation and planning for VIP visits, working with other agencies and range work. At the end of the course was a scenario which involved a visit by a VIP, where Aidrian and his fellow students planned and executed a visit to various locations within the area.

The part of the VIP in the scenario was played by one of West Yorkshire's Assistant Chief Constables and during the latter half of the exercise there was simulated attack on the vehicle convoy, where the principle's vehicle became boxed in. During this scenario, Aidrian was sitting next to the Assistant Chief Constable. Without thinking about it, and acting purely on instinct, Aidrian quickly removed the VIP from the rear of their vehicle and did not stand on ceremony in doing it, pushing open the door and dragging him out, causing him to land in a muddy ditch minus one of his shoes and several buttons from his shirt. Aidrian successfully passed the course, despite leaving his mark on a somewhat dishevelled and muddy Assistant Chief Constable. His shooting results over the range workdays was a staggering 99%: the highest score ever achieved up to that point.

To keep up to date with what was happening in the 'real world', all firearms instructors were 'on call' so that they could be used for live operations on a rotating basis. If they were not used within the actual team, they would observe the operation, watching how officers performed, and bring any problems or positives that had arisen into later training scenarios, for everybody's benefit.

During Aidrian's time as an instructor, Essex Police changed their weaponry from .38 Smith & Wesson revolvers to the 9-mm Beretta, and the .223 Ruger rifles to the Heckler & Koch 9-mm carbine. One of the advantages of this change was that both the new weapons used the exact same ammunition and provided all Essex police firearms officers with increased firepower, as well as better safety factors. Aidrian and his fellow instructors had the somewhat unenviable task of having to instruct all of Essex Police's firearms officers on the conversion over to the new weapons, which involved a great deal of work, as everyone had to requalify before their firearms permits could be updated and they were authorised to carry and use the new weaponry.

The *Manual of Guidance on Police Use of Firearms* advocated tactics that were predominantly defensive in their actions. All firearms officers were not taught aggressive forced entry and assault tactics as it was presumed that if such methods were ever required, the military would be called in. If such a requirement was ever deemed necessary, it would be a decision made by senior officers.

Aidrian, along with other instructors from several forces across the country, felt there was a gap in the tactical ability of firearms officers to be able to deal effectively with certain situations that could develop rapidly during a live operation. Such a scenario may not have been considered a military matter, or if it was, it simply was not feasible to wait for the military to arrive due to the potential loss of life if matters were not dealt with expediently by the officers at the scene.

To this end, Aidrian produced an in-depth report based on this potential scenario and approval was given for an element of training in assault tactics to several suitable officers of the Tactical Firearms Group. It became known as intervention training. One of the Essex Police firearms instructors had contacts with elements of the military who were knowledgeable about these types of tactics, and he was able to arrange for a number of the instructors to undergo training to an efficient enough standard that they were then in turn able to train other officers within Essex.

After all members of the Tactical Firearms Group had completed a training module based on these new tactics, two of the firearms instructors selected suitable officers to be fully trained. I was one of the officers who took part in the training module but was not one of those selected to be trained up. The training was agreed at senior level within Essex Police and resulted in two courses going ahead, each of which lasted for two weeks, with a dozen members of the Tactical Firearms Group on each of the courses.

In essence, this new type of training allowed the police to enter buildings in an offensive manner in situations such as a

Above left: Essex Police firearms officers enjoying some down time on Blue Peter in the Doctor Who Tardis at the BBC TV studios in London.

Above right: The author wearing camouflage gear. I was on a nighttime exercise on a military training base somewhere in the UK.

Confiscated and recovered illegal firearms.

Above left: Greater Manchester Police Firearms patch.

Above right: City of London Firearms patch.

Police firearms officers undergoing training scenarios.

Right: A police firearms officer taking part in a live operation.

Below: Image of two CTSFOs showing the numerous pieces of equipment they need to wear.

COUNTER-TERRORISM SPECIALIST FIREARMS OFFICER: THE KIT

RIFLE
Precision tactical rifle

COMBAT HELMET & GOtGGLES
Helmet able to stop close-range bullets

BODY ARMOUR
Kevlar/ceramic to stop bullets

PISTOL
Reliable & accurate Glock 17

TASER
Incapacitate suspect, with output of up to 50,000 volts

FLAME-RETARDENT OVERALLS
Fire-proof knee & elbow pads

A Heckler & Koch G36C carbine/assault rifle with a 30 x 5.56-mm round magazine.

A Heckler & Koch MP5 carbine with 30 x 9-mm round magazine used by several police forces in the UK.

Above: An officer carrying a Sig Sauer SG516 semi-automatic carbine/rifle with a 30 x 5.56-mm round magazine.

Left: The author wearing a beret, newly issued style coveralls and carrying a Heckler & Koch MP5 carbine on a training day in Colchester, Essex.

ESSEX POLICE
FIREARMS PERMIT

No. 501

Pc 2012 S J WYNN

is hereby authorised to carry
.38 Revolvers

for operational purposes until the date of expiry shown overleaf

Chief Constable

Date 26.8.88

The author's first firearms permit issued in 1988, showing the firearm he was initially authorised to carry for operational police purposes.

Above: A hi-jacking incident at Stansted Airport in 1996. The author is stood immediately at the top of the stairs just prior to boarding the aircraft.

Right: The author and a colleague at Stansted Airport on 2 August 1990, the first day of the Gulf War. The airport was designated to deal with all returning British casualties.

The author stood in front of an armoured Land Rover, carrying a Heckler & Koch MP5 carbine, outside the old Force Support Unit building in Chelmsford, 1997.

Above left: The author guarding the late Queen at the opening of the Bell Tower at St Martins Church, Basildon, 12 March 1999.

Above right: In August 1984, Brian 'Bill' Bishop was the last Essex Police firearms officer to be shot and killed on duty, after attempting to arrest an armed suspect. Bill is seen here at Stansted Airport in June 1983, when the American space shuttle *Enterprise* came to the UK on its way home from that year's Paris air show.

Counter Terrorism Specialist Firearms Officers, the highest level of firearms officer in the UK, undergoing training scenarios. All the officers are wearing gas masks, and in the first two images, notice how the last man is armed with a baton gun and not a carbine.

Above: Two police firearms officers carry out the arrest of an individual at the end of a training hijacking incident.

Left: A police firearms officer taking aim at a suspect from behind the safety of their own police vehicle during a training exercise.

Below: The Ford Jankel Guardian armoured vehicles weigh 7 tonnes, have solid rubber tyres, a 6-litre engine and have enough room for eight officers and their equipment. They are used by a number of police forces throughout the UK.

hostage rescue scenario, where it was felt that a person's life was at imminent danger. As an example of this, Aidrian was one of the Essex Police firearms officers who entered White House Farm near the village of Tolleshunt D'Arcy on 7 August 1985 to carry out a search of the premises. Aidrian and his colleagues discovered the bodies of Nevil and June Bamber, their adopted daughter, Sheila Caffell, and her 6-year-old twin sons, Daniel and Nicholas. Back in 1985, however, there was no such thing as counselling for firearms officers or taking time out for a week to emotionally recover. It was straight back to work the very next day, as it had been for Aidrian and his colleagues the day after their friend and colleague, Brian Bishop, had been killed the previous year. But despite this, events such as these had a lasting effect on all concerned. They were never forgotten.

Aidrian recalls how he always told students on the first day of their basic firearms course to make sure they had discussed with their loved ones the potential enormity of the course they were about to undertake. He felt that it was important that their wives, husbands and/or family needed to know and understand that once they had passed their course and qualified as an operational police firearms officer, their actions, once deployed, may result in their death or the death of another. If an officer had not had such a conversation, then Aidrian politely suggested that such a course was not really for them, and that the door was open for them to leave without them having any feeling of shame or having failed. Despite having mentioned this at the beginning of each and every basic course he was involved with, Aidrian cannot recall anyone taking up the option to leave, but he did feel on some occasions that during the course, some officers clearly had not fully thought through the implications of what they were about to embark upon. This was born out when some officers voluntarily left their courses early, whilst others were failed for various different reasons.

Always one for a new challenge, Aidrian transferred from the Weapons Training department to Special Branch, who were based at Stansted Airport, in 1992, taking his close protection training and knowledge with him.

During his time as a firearms permit holder for Essex Police, Aidrian was deployed on hundreds of operations. He and his colleagues had a mantra that said a successful firearms operation was one where no shots were fired by anybody, no one was hurt and at the end of the day, we all went home to our families and loved ones.

This excellent insight into the work life of a firearms officer allows us to fully understand just how professional and dedicated police firearms officers are. It also shows that from generation to generation, the experience passed on from firearms instructors to their students is of the highest possible quality and is based on years and years of personal experience, honed to perfection through the knowledge gathered as a result of having been deployed on hundreds of firearms operations.

It is only right to finish this chapter by allowing Aidrian to describe in his own words the memory of one particular firearms operation he took part in, sometime during the mid to late 1980s.

Working on information from Essex Police's Drug Squad, and continuing intelligence, we discovered that there was a boat arriving at a particular point along the River Thames, with a cargo of a large amount of cannabis on board, and that those on board the boat may well be in possession of firearms. The problem we had was we did not know the exact location of where the boat in question would land. A number of my colleagues and I were deployed to what was then known as Laindon Traffic Garage. That same evening, we received information that the boat we were expecting was sailing along the River Thames, and that we needed to be ready just in case it stopped in Essex.

During the course of the night, we were told that it had somehow managed to get stuck on a sandbank, and that with the tide out, it wasn't going anywhere until there was a tide change, which would lift it off the sandbank. Despite the excitement and anticipation of forthcoming events, all we could do was to get our heads down and have a sleep. The next morning the incoming tide lifted the boat off the sandbank and once again, it was on the move. By this time, we had been on duty for somewhere in the region of about sixteen hours, so we made a request to be relieved, only to be told that the only other available firearms officers had been deployed in relation to another live operation, and there wasn't anyone else at this stage available to take over from us.

In the end the boat passed straight through Essex and docked in East London, without stopping. 'Great,' we thought to ourselves, 'over to the Mets, and we can all go home and have a much-needed sleep.' No such luck. Before we got too excited, we were informed that the Metropolitan Police firearms unit was involved in another operation and needed us to make our way to a location in East London, where exactly, I cannot now remember, to attend a briefing. So, we packed up all our kit and equipment, and off we went to East London.

The result was that firearms officers from the Metropolitan Police were going to carry out a 'strike' on the boat after it had unloaded its cargo onto a van that was waiting on the quay side, but not before the van left. Our job was to make our way to the van's final destination and to arrest anybody we found there.

With the van finally loaded up with its narcotic style cargo, it left the dock area and made its way to an archway lock-up, under a railway bridge in East London. We were hastily briefed and guided to the location where an armour-plated forklift truck, which was owned by the Metropolitan Police, drove through the front doors of the lock-up, hastily followed by myself and the other members of our team. We arrested four men who were inside the lock-up at gun point, and who were in possession of several large bails of cannabis. By this time, we had been on duty for approximately thirty hours. To make matters *even worse, if that was possible, a colleague and I were instructed to stay behind to secure the cannabis until members of the Metropolitan Police's Scenes of Crime department arrived.*

I have often wondered what would have happened if the operation had turned out differently and shots had been fired, what the subsequent enquiry would have said in relation to the number of hours we had all been on duty. Thankfully we will never know. I certainly don't think the same would happen today as there are a lot more police officers trained in the use of firearms.

The years I spent as a firearms officer with Essex Police, were the best time of my policing career. I would do it all again in a heartbeat.

Aidrian retired in 2002, having served in the Essex Police for thirty years. Due to his wealth of experience and knowledge in the field of police firearms operations and training, he then acted as a civilian consultant to assist in the writing of an exercise portraying a terrorist hi-jacking at Stansted Airport, to help test the military, government, police and all the country's security agencies. The exercise took approximately a year to put together, then a further nine months to write up, following all the numerous recommendations.

CHAPTER FOURTEEN

Armed Robbers and Robberies During the 1960s and 1970s

Armed robberies, either on banks or on vehicles carrying cash to and from banks, were regular targets for members of the criminal fraternity throughout the 1960s and 1970s, with the potential to make those taking part in such heists very rich individuals. Along with a black balaclava and a stolen getaway car, the weapon of choice for these robbers was either a pistol or a double-barrelled sawn-off shotgun, which in the wrong hands could be devastating. Looks can be deceiving, however, because no criminal really wants to pull the trigger of his gun and, in the process, kill an innocent member of the public, but they certainly do want to frighten the hell out of people and make sure that nobody suddenly decides they want to be a hero.

For those who chose to 'earn their living' as an armed bank robber in the 1960s and 1970s, very large sums of money could be obtained, with the person knowing full well there was little in place to prevent them from being successful. They also became the celebrities of the criminal underworld.

The other aspect that must be taken into consideration with this subject, is, of course, police corruption. Things finally became so bad that in 1978, Home Secretary Merlyn Rees ordered an investigation under the name of Operation Countryman, which eventually resulted in eight police officers being charged and prosecuted, although none of them was convicted. The investigation began after an unnamed informant had made allegations that certain officers within the City of London Police, and from the Metropolitan Police's elite Flying Squad, who were responsible for dealing with armed robberies, had taken bribes, fabricated evidence against certain individuals, and had arranged for charges against criminals to be dropped. On 7 July 1977, the Flying Squad's commander, Detective Chief Superintendent Ken Drury, had been convicted on five counts of corruption and sent to prison for eight years. Other members of the squad were put on trial and convicted, whilst others resigned, realising that it was in their best interests to do so.

The banks themselves were relatively easy targets, largely because they really did not help themselves. There were no armed guards or security cameras, and even their internal layout was not designed or built with security in mind. The police also had no helicopters, nor did every street corner have numerous different types of CCTV systems hanging from a telegraph pole. Most importantly, however, there were no police firearms units waiting for the criminals as they came rushing out of the bank. Although the British police did have access to guns throughout the 1960s and 1970s, there were no highly trained SWAT teams in place, nor was there any tactical thinking to deal with such scenarios. The most the police had was a few divisional officers and senior Constables, or those who had previously served in the military in some capacity who, if the circumstances deemed it necessary, would be called back to the station to collect a gun. That was it. That was as much as the police use of firearms stretched to.

Armed robberies declined overtime, not because the robbers became older, but because security started to improve. Security vans that were laden with cash had devices placed between some of the bundles which in certain circumstances would 'explode' and give off a blue dye which would stain the banknotes, in effect making them worthless, along with the skin of anybody caught in its wake.

The police service as a whole certainly looked at their own firearms capability, including the number of men they had trained in the use of firearms and tactics, and the types of weapons and ammunition they used. Suddenly, carrying out armed robberies was not that straight forward anymore and they simply became too risky. With the numbers of police officers being trained in the use of firearms, it meant there was more of a chance of criminals being confronted by armed police officers, which was a no-win situation. On the one hand there was more chance of them being shot, and if they shot a police officer whilst trying to escape, any prison sentence would no doubt see them spend the best years of their life behind bars. The chances of getting caught increased, which meant if found guilty at court, they would more than likely face an extremely heavy prison sentence. Suddenly, robbing banks did not have the same appeal anymore.

It was not just the police who understood they had to employ different tactics if they wanted to prevent and deter criminals from continuing to rob banks. One of the ways the banks chose to combat this at the time was to reduce the number of branches. It was simple economics. The fewer banks there were, the fewer could be robbed.

As the years have moved on, so has the world. Nothing ever stays the same and even robbers have been part of that evolution. The carrying of a firearm whilst carrying out a crime has attracted a much stiffer prison sentence, regardless of whether it was used in the execution of the crime. To a large degree this has caused criminals to look at their actions, so that if they do get caught, the chances are they would receive a lesser prison sentence.

With the explosion of the internet in recent years, for those criminals who are more technically minded, they do not even have to leave the comfort of their own homes. They can simply sit in front of a computer and commit acts of fraud, which can potentially bring them in large sums of money, with little or no chance of ever being caught.

CHAPTER FIFTEEN

The Shepherd's Bush Murders, 1966

The story of the Shepherd's Bush Murders is an important one as it was undoubtedly the catalyst which led to police forces up and down the country taking the issue around their role in the use of firearms more seriously. Thanks to this incident, police forces nationwide considered changing from simply having guns locked away in police stations only issued to older, more experienced officers, or those with previous military experience, to use as and when needed, to seriously considering having specially trained officers and units to deal with such incidents. Rather than just reacting in an ad hoc manner, there was a realisation that a much more professional response was needed. As a result of the cold-blooded murder of the three Metropolitan Police officers, senior police officers recognised simply issuing firearms to a selected number of frontline officers who just happened to be on duty at the time of a firearms related incident, was no longer acceptable.

The Shepherd's Bush Murders, or the Massacre of Braybrook Street, took place on Friday, 12 August 1966, and resulted in the deaths of three young police officers: Police Constable Geoffrey Roger Fox, Detective Sergeant Christopher Tippett Head and Temporary Detective Constable David S. Bertram Wombwell. The three police officers had stopped to question three men sat in a car in Braybrook Street, not far from Wormwood Scrubs prison. The three men in the car were petty criminals Harry Maurice Roberts, John Duddy and John Edward Witney.

At approximately 3:15pm on the Friday afternoon, the three plain-clothed police officers were patrolling in the East Acton area of London in an unmarked Triumph 2000 police Q-car with the call-sign of Foxtrot One One. DS Head and TDC Wombwell were both members of the Criminal Investigation Department, stationed at Shepherd's Bush police station, whilst PC Fox was a divisional beat officer who regularly acted as a Q-car driver due to his wide-ranging knowledge of both the local area and the local criminals. As Fox drove into Braybrook Street, he and his colleagues spotted a pale, blue-coloured Standard Vanguard Estate van parked further up the road. The car had seen better days and stuck out even more because it was not displaying the required tax disc along the bottom of the windscreen. Fox stopped the car and Head and Wombwell got out and walked across to the van. The driver was John Witney; the front seat passenger was Harry Roberts and sat in the rear of the vehicle was John Duddy. After introducing themselves as police officers, Head enquired why the vehicle was not displaying a tax disc, to which Witney replied that he was waiting for his MOT certificate, which was needed before road tax could be applied for. Head then asked to see Witney's driving licence, which he produced. He then asked for his insurance for the vehicle and on checking it noticed that it had expired at noon that day. Head then asked Wombwell to write down Witney's details and having done so, he walked around to the passenger side of the vehicle. Witney and Wombwell got into a conversation about how Witney had only been reported for the same offence just a couple of weeks earlier.

Without any warning, Roberts, who was the front seat passenger, leant across Witney and aimed a German Luger pistol at Wombwell.

He pulled the trigger and shot him once in the face, with the bullet passing through his left eye and killing him instantly. In a state of shock, Head began running back towards Fox and the Q-car, but Roberts was quickly out of his seat and chased after him. He fired twice. The first shot missed, whilst the second struck him in the back. Roberts tried to shoot the fallen officer again, but his gun jammed, not once, but twice. Duddy, who was armed with a armed forces-issued .38 Webley service revolver, had been sat in the rear of the vehicle and now followed Roberts along the road towards the police Q-car. At the same time, Fox, in what can only be described as an act of extreme bravery, decided to reverse his vehicle at speed towards Roberts and Duddy, the latter of whom fired three shots at Fox through the front passenger window of the Q-car. Miraculously, the first two shots missed before the third struck Fox in the right side of his temple. As he died, Fox's right foot pushed down on the accelerator pedal, causing the vehicle to run over the body of DS Head.

After having shot all three police officers, Roberts and Duddy got back into their van, and Witney drove off at speed. Fortunately, a passer-by was drawn to the vehicle because of its erratic speed so close to Wormwood Scrubs prison, and wrote down the vehicle's registration number, which showed that it was owned by John Witney. Whitney returned to his home within hours of the killings and when police called at his address that evening, he claimed that he had sold the car earlier in the day to somebody he did not know. Police found the car the following day in a lock-up that was rented by Witney in Lambeth. Three .38 calibre live rounds of ammunition were discovered in the vehicle and Witney was arrested on suspicion of murder.

The old saying that there is no honour amongst thieves was quickly proven when Witney wasted no time in giving up the names of his two accomplices, Duddy and Roberts. The former was arrested on 17 August, hiding up in a tenement block in Glasgow, whilst Roberts managed to stay at large for a total of ninety-six days before he was captured in Bishop Stortford, Hertfordshire.

Roberts and Witney had previously carried out various armed robberies on betting shops, banks and building societies, before Duddy had come along and joined the gang. The reason why the shootings took place was because the men, who were in the process of planning their next armed robbery, were worried that the police would search the vehicle and find their stash of weapons in a holdall on the back seat, next to Duddy.

What shocked the police and the general public about this particular incident was its brutality and callousness. The murders took place just eight months after the death penalty in England, Wales and Scotland was suspended following the Murder (Abolition of Death Penalty) Act 1965 and instead replaced with a mandatory sentence of life imprisonment.

All three men stood trial at the Central Criminal Court at the Old Bailey on 12 December 1966. The trial last for six days. Roberts pleaded guilty to all charges against him, other than the murder of PC Geoffrey Fox. Duddy's defence team tried to place the blame on Roberts and Witney, whilst his legal team put the blame on Duddy and Roberts. All three men were found guilty. Roberts of the murders of Head and Wombwell, and Duddy of the murder of Fox. In Roberts' case, the judge, Mr Justice Glyn-Jones, recommended that all three men should serve a minimum of thirty years' imprisonment before they were considered for parole. Roberts eventually served forty-eight years in prison before being released on parole on 11 November 2014, at the age of 78. Even after serving such a long sentence, opinion was divided as to whether he should have been released. Certainly, the relatives of the murdered officers and the Police Federation of England and Wales were against it.

Duddy died in Parkhurst prison on 8 December 1981, While Witney was released from prison in 1991, having served only twenty-five years of his recommended thirty-year sentence. He was bludgeoned to death with a hammer by his heroin addicted flatmate in August 1999.

Following the murders, in November 1967 Lord Hamilton, the MP for Fermanagh and South Tyrone, asked the British Home Secretary whether the government would consider supplying British police officers with electric truncheons to maintain law and order. Lord Hamilton explained how such batons, a British invention, were used in America. In an effort to support his request, he added that experts had stated the Shepherd's Bush murders might not have been committed if the police had been armed with such truncheons. However, Lord Hamilton did not explain how exactly any of the officers would have avoided being shot, if they had been in possession of an electric baton.

CHAPTER SIXTEEN

The Clydesdale Bank Robbery, 1969

This is quite possibly one of the saddest accounts of the murder of police officers there has ever been.

On Tuesday, 30 December 1969, three smartly dressed men arrived at a branch of the Clydesdale Bank in Bridge Street, Linwood, Scotland, for a 3pm appointment with the branch manager, Mr Flemming, to discuss opening an account for a new plant hire business. On arrival, they were taken to the manager's officer by a Mr Mackin, the bank's accountant. As soon as they entered the office the three men pushed Mackin to the floor and he was then threatened by two of the men, with one holding a pistol to his head and the other, a knife to his throat. Mackin was then informed that if he co-operated, none of the staff would be harmed. A pillowcase was then placed over his head and his hands were tied behind his back. When Mr Flemming returned to his office a short while later, he immediately had a gun placed against the back of his neck. The rest of the bank's staff, as well as the customers who were also in the bank, were also herded into the same office.

The three men proceeded to fill several suitcases with money from the bank's safe, which was open, and from an unlocked counter drawer. The three men then calmly left the bank, but not before they had threatened their hostages, who they locked in the manager's office, telling them not to sound the alarm for five minutes until after they had gone. Their getaway car, waiting for them outside the front of the bank, took them to an address in Allison Street, Glasgow. The men had escaped with approximately £14,000, which in today's money would be somewhere in the region of £288,000.

The distance between the bank and Allison Street is approximately 8.5 miles, with a travelling time of less than twenty minutes.

At about 4:25pm the three men, having already removed all the bank notes from the car and taken them into 51 Allison Street, returned to the car to collect the large amount of coinage they had also stolen from the bank. It was whilst carrying the money in large suitcases and a black box that they came to the attention of Police Inspector Andrew Hyslop and Police Constable John Sellars of the City of Glasgow Police. Not only was it a complete coincidence that the two police officers were in Allison Street, but they also knew nothing about the robbery which had taken place earlier that afternoon at the Clydesdale Bank. Suspecting that the men might be dealing in illicit whisky, Hyslop decided to leave PC Sellars to keep watch on the address while he drove to the nearby police station to get assistance.

Whilst Hyslop was away, one of the three men, 31-year-old Howard Wilson, came out of the house and engaged Sellars in conversation, stating that he owned a shop in Mount Florida, and was popping out to get some lemonade from a nearby shop. A short while later, Hyslop returned with Police Constable John Campbell, acting Detective Constable Angus MacKenzie and Constable Edward Barnett, all of whom were in plain clothes.

When Wilson returned from the shop, he was questioned by Hyslop about the heavy suitcases he had been seen removing from the car. Wilson was polite and co-operative and invited the police officers to his home so they could see for themselves. Once inside he remained calm, even offering them a cup of tea. At one point in the proceedings, Hyslop went into another room and found one of the men, 22-year-old John Sim, sat on a suitcase with another by his feet. Hyslop opened the suitcase that was on the floor only to discover it contained bags with the name 'Linwood' on the side and with money inside them. At this point, the third man, 31-year-old Ian Donaldson, left the house but was stopped and brought back to the house.

Hyslop enquired as to the location of the black box, and when none of the three men was forthcoming with its location, Hyslop and his men began searching the house. Sellars and Hyslop went upstairs and looked in the bathroom, whilst Campbell remained with Sim and the two suitcases, and began questioning him, whilst Donaldson and Wilson left the room. As it turned out, Donaldson left the house whilst Wilson went upstairs into one of the bedrooms. Having finished searching the bathroom, Hyslop stepped out onto the landing to be confronted by Wilson holding a pistol in his right hand, which he was pointing at Hyslop's head. Without any words between the two men, Wilson pulled the trigger, but there was only a click, indicating that the pistol had jammed. Undeterred, he managed to unclear the obstruction and despite Hyslop rushing at him, Wilson managed to fire the weapon; the round striking Hyslop on the left side of his face, the force knocking him to the floor.

Wilson then started making his way downstairs. The noise of the gunfire had drawn Mackenzie into the hallway and Barnett towards the doorway of the kitchen. Wilson took aim again, firstly at MacKenzie and then Barnett, striking both men in the head. Barnett died five days later in hospital.

Wilson then went back upstairs and, stepping over Hyslop, tried to get into the bathroom where Sellars had taken refuge and was trying to summon help via his personal radio. Whilst he was doing this, Wilson managed to get the door partially open, but luckily for Sellars, he could not get his gun round far enough to fire at him. At about the same time, Wilson saw Hyslop, who he assumed was dead, move slightly, so he pointed his weapon at his head, but before he could pull the trigger, Campbell, who had made his way upstairs, flung himself at Wilson and both men fell to the floor. In the ensuing tussle, Campbell managed to get hold of the barrel of the gun. The two men continued to struggle and eventually Campbell managed to get control of the weapon, allowing him to lead Wilson and Sim out into the street. Fortunately for Campbell, two uniformed officers happened to be walking past, and Sim and Wilson were detained and taken into custody.

It would appear that Sim had no idea Wilson had any intention of shooting the officers, and during the incident Wilson asked him to go to the car outside and get some more ammunition, but Sim had refused to do so.

As for Wilson, it was clear from his actions that he had not shot any of the police officers to escape, but purely with the intention of killing them.

Donaldson, who had left before any of the police officers had been shot, was arrested at his home later that evening.

The three men went to trial the following February, where they appeared before Judge Lord Hall at the Edinburgh court and were all found guilty as charged. In dealing with Wilson, Hall told him that the only sentence he could give was life imprisonment with a recommendation that he serve a minimum of twenty-five years before he was considered for release. Wilson also received a further twelve-year sentence for the armed robbery, but this was to be served concurrent with his life sentence. In the cases of Sim and Donaldson, both men were found guilty of the armed robbery and given twelve-year prison sentences.

What made this case even more galling, if that were even possible, was the fact that Wilson and Sim were both ex-police officers, yet despite this, Wilson had taken the lives of two police officers without an apparent care in the world.

It was tragic set of circumstances which had resulted in Hyslop and his men coming into contact with Wilson, Sim and Donaldson, but one which may not have happened if the officers had been armed or had known of the armed robbery that had previously taken place at Linwood. In the end, the officers had assumed they were dealing with nothing more sinister than three men who were involved in dealing with stolen liquor.

CHAPTER SEVENTEEN

The Ramsey Incident, 1979

The first time police officers in Essex had to discharge a firearm operationally was in March 1979, when 18-year-old Paul Howe was shot dead by police outside the Castle pub in Ramsey, near Harwich. The officer who fired the fatal shot was a member of the Force Support Unit. Howe had been due to appear at Northampton Magistrates' Court earlier in the month but had failed to turn up and so a warrant had been issued for his arrest.

On the evening of Tuesday, 20 March 1979 an incident took place which resulted in a 23-year-old man being taken hostage by Howe in Chelmsford, Essex. A high-speed chase then followed, taking them across the county to Colchester and on to Harwich Docks, where Howe and his hostage briefly boarded a container ship, before commandeering a police transit van and leaving the dock area. During this time, Howe fired a number of shots before continuing on his way and eventually arriving at the Castle pub, where he fired two more shots. On entering the pub, he allowed most of the customers to leave, subsequently releasing the remaining hostages, except the original man he had taken hostage in Chelmsford.

A reporter telephoned the pub and spoke with Howe, who told him: 'If they want me, they're going to have to kill me to take me.'

During the night, Howe appeared much calmer and began building up a rapport with the hostage.

Just before 6:30am the following morning, Howe fired more shots, and smoke and flames were seen coming from inside the pub. It was soon after this that the hostage managed to escape. It was not much later that Howe came out of the pub firing a shotgun. The police returned fire, and Howe was fatally struck in the chest. One of the shots fired by Howe had struck a police officer in the head, leaving him with a minor wound.

It is always a sad time when anybody loses their life in such circumstances. Below is a letter written to *The Law* newspaper by Matt Comrie, who at the time of the incident was an Assistant Chief Constable (ACC) with Essex Police and the duty ACC at the time of the shooting. The letter was published in the newspaper's edition of April 1979.

> Dear Sir,
>
> Until last Wednesday morning our Force, despite hundreds of incidents, had preserved a proud record of not having fired in an operational situation. That record ended in the tragic death of Paul Howe. It is a situation none of us relish.
>
> A small section of the press were unhappy and even misleading. They will be answered in due course at the inquest. The due process of law must be observed by the officers directly involved and statements cannot be made at this time. However, some remarks can be commented upon by me: for example, the woman reporter of a Sunday newspaper who wrote, 'there is something not quite right about the whole story,' among other rather childlike comments.

It is unfortunate that the lady was not at the incident, neither did she attend any of the press conferences. We all share her unhappiness with the ills of society, if that is what she meant to say.

The same newspaper company carried the suggestion that crack units from the Metropolitan Police, with superior equipment, should have been called in. Apart from the fact there are no 'crack units', whatever that term meant to convey, we in Essex Police know what is available from the Met's and our other Police neighbours, and we are not shy if we need help.

Mr Price, the DCC, was at the front line and will in consequence answer HM Coroner's questions, but I as duty ACC on that day can assure your readers that the whole force responded to the emergency with policeman ship of the highest order. The Force Support Unit cannot be bettered for discipline, bearing and conduct. Our Firearms Unit is second to none. We shall of course learn from the experience, but the Chief Officers of the Force are satisfied that training and previous operational experience stood us in good stead on this occasion.

Our Police Authority have never been stinting in the provision of the equipment we need and ask for. The Met could not in these circumstances have provided more or better.

It was unfortunate that Jim Jardine used the words he did when he spoke, albeit off the cuff, to the press, but I share his sentiments, we do not like our finger on the trigger.

It is very sad that the incident did not end without the loss of life. We may have to face the same situation again. Society must realise they have placed their Police in a difficult and dangerous position.

Yours faithfully
M D Comrie

The following was an editorial that appeared in the very same newspaper:

A sad statistic, one out of one

Was any other outcome possible at the Ramsey siege? The do-gooders who specialise in wisdom after the event will dream up possibilities but there was an awful inevitability about the train of events.

Never before had Essex Police needed to open fire in any situation in the County and on this occasion forebore from shooting back until forced by circumstances to discharge one gun: a sad statistic, one out of one.

There has to be a first time for everything, thereafter the medicine is easier to swallow. And there lies the danger which every member of the Force should recognise, fear and guard against attractions of imposing censorship upon this column, went on to tell him that if he thought The Law was widely read he was living in Cloud Cuckoo land, a phrase we recognise from somewhere, though we would have thought that if few read it censorship would be an empty gesture. Then constable's refresher course made menacing noises about our sentiments, telling a senior officer that they wouldn't read this column anymore until we agreed with them: illogical maybe but effective.

So, we have achieved the accolade of annoying both extremes of the rank structure which, on second thoughts, must be an acceptance of a sort.

It is always an interest to me to read the language of the day in connection with such incidents. For a start, not only do we have a factual article that recounts the story as it should be told, honestly, but one that has a real feel to it. A vibrancy, if you will.

One of the officers who was involved in the Ramsey Incident was PC John Manners, who retired from Essex Police in 1997. His last posting had been as a member of the Weapons Training Department, back in 1979, and he had previously been a member of the FSU. I had known John from my own time on the unit when he was also part of the Weapons Training Department. He was also immediately in front of me on the steps of the aircraft during the Sudan Airways hijacking in 1996.

I contacted John to see if he would give me his recollection of the event on that day back in April 1979. What follows is his personal account:

As I recall my shift started about 6am on that fateful day.

For me it was a short journey into the office. Our original duty for the day was just routine and nothing particularly out of the ordinary. We were deployed on plain clothes observation duties near Passingford Bridge, Stondon Massey, and Ongar, logging certain motor vehicles.

At some point during the day, we were informed over the radio (this was long before the invention of mobile phones) of a firearms incident that had started in Chelmsford, when local CID officers had tried to arrest a person by the name of Paul Howe for drugs-related offences. At the time I had never heard of him, nor knew nothing about him.

I'm not totally certain of the exact sequence of events, but originally, he made off from the officers and it was quickly determined that he was in possession of an air rifle. He somehow managed to take a passing motorist or neighbour, I'm not sure which, hostage in his car and made off in the general direction of the A12.

We were told to stop the operation we had originally been deployed on and return to HQ to draw our firearms. We were then informed that Howe and the hostage were being followed along the A12 towards Colchester by two officers from the FSU, plus CID officers from Chelmsford. As soon as we had been issued with our firearms, we were immediately mobilised, but by now were still quite some distance behind Howe and the pursuing officers.

Howe eventually turned off the A12 and drove all the way to Harwich Docks. On route he had been firing at the tyres of lorries he had overtaken, presumably to make them crash in order to hold up the following police vehicles. On arriving at the docks, Howe and his hostage abandoned their vehicle and managed to get on board a cargo ship of some considerable size that was docked there. He apparently made efforts to start the ship but was, of course, unable to do so. How he thought he was going to get the ship started or where he was intending to go, I have no idea.

Several police transit vans had by now arrived and deployed both armed and unarmed men on foot in the area immediately near to where the ship was berthed.

After a short while, Howe realised that he was not going to be able start the ship and escape across the seas, so he got off, but unfortunately for us, he was still with his hostage. He made his way to the dock entrance on foot, managing to keep us at bay by using his hostage.

Many of the police transits which had arrived earlier at the scene to deploy officers were still parked at the entrance of the docks and *unfortunately, Howe found one of them with the keys still in the ignition. This of course he took full advantage of and, by forcing the hostage to drive them both out of the docks, eventually headed towards Ramsey. We all got back into our vehicles and followed after them in hot pursuit.*

As you are now aware, Howe ended up at the local pub in Ramsey. All attempts by the police to negotiate with him up to this time he had completely ignored, and no attempts were made by the police to open fire because of the potential danger this would cause to the hostage.

If my memory serves me correctly, Howe, his hostage and the police all arrived at the pub sometime after 7pm that evening. Howe entered the pub, which had many customers in it at the time. We very quickly contained the immediate area with armed officers, and there was also an outer cordon of unarmed officers. I remember that the media, press and TV were all very quickly on scene as well.

I can't quite remember how it came about, but Howe had somehow managed to acquire himself a shotgun and some ammunition for it. I think the shotgun belonged to the landlord of the pub. I also seem to recall that Howe had been speaking to the media via telephone.

At some time during the siege, several customers who had been hiding in the pub's toilets managed to escape and were led to safety. Howe didn't know this had happened. Negotiations were on going via a telephone link, and eventually all the hostages were released with the exception of the original one.

Throughout the course of the night and early morning, Howe fired indiscriminatingly from time to time at the containment officers and unfortunately for one FSU officer, Graham Harvey, he was hit in the head by shotgun pellets whilst taking cover behind a parked vehicle at the front of the pub. Thankfully for all concerned, his injuries were not life threatening.

Because the situation was on-going and drawn out, replacement officers had to be called up, with many coming straight from their homes to the scene. There were simply not enough firearms to go round as most of them were already on scene. Plans were made to deploy officers to certain positions so they could take weapons over from other officers if the situation suddenly deteriorated rapidly.

I can't remember exactly when, but the last remaining hostage, the original one Howe had taken back in Chelmsford, managed to escape. This obviously must have annoyed Howe as he then proceeded to set fire to the pub.

After a while it started to get too hot and smoky in the pub, so Howe then came out into the back garden and sat down. He still had the shotgun with him. He was continually challenged by officers but ignored all pleas to put the gun down. At one point he raised the gun, and an officer fired at him but missed.

Howe then stood up and walked out of the garden, making directly towards the containment officers at the front of the pub. I should have mentioned earlier that the pub was in the middle of a housing estate, which made the situation potentially even more dangerous. As Howe walked across the car park at the front of the pub, he was holding the shotgun across his chest and continued to ignore all pleas to stop.

The same officer who had earlier fired and missed, fired another shot which struck Howe in the chest. He fell to the ground, dropping the gun in the process and a number of us immediately moved towards him to administer first aid. A short while later he was placed in a waiting ambulance and taken to hospital, where he later died.

By the end of the siege, many of us had been on duty in excess of 24 hours without a break, but talking it over amongst ourselves later, we all found it very difficult to sleep and I don't think that we fully recovered until about a week later.

CHAPTER EIGHTEEN

The Shooting of Stephen Waldorf, 1983

On 14 January 1983, an incident took place in London which resulted in the shooting by police officers of 26-year-old Stephen Waldorf. The shooting was notable for several reasons, including the issuing of new guidelines for the police and their use of firearms, not just for the Metropolitan Police, but for all police forces throughout the UK. In essence, the rules and regulations concerning when police could use firearms, who could use them and who could issue them, were greatly tightened up.

Stephen Waldorf was shot and seriously injured after the police had mistaken him for David Martin; an escaped criminal who was into cross-dressing and was considered to be an extremely dangerous individual. Martin had repeatedly used violence to resist arrest and had previously escaped custody, or attempted to escape, on more than one occasion. He had served a nine-year prison sentence, starting in 1973, for a series of frauds and burglaries. His sentence was originally eight years, but he received an extra year for his role in a prison escape. He was released in 1981 and resumed his criminal career, committing a series of burglaries, including one in July 1982 in which he stole twenty-four pistols and almost 1,000 rounds of ammunition from a gun shop. From then on, Martin carried two guns wherever he went. He committed armed robberies with the guns and ammunition he had stolen, and on one of the robberies he showed he was not to be reckoned with when he shot and wounded a security guard. In August 1982, police officers caught Martin in the act of burgling a recording studio, but he shot his way out, seriously injuring one of the officers in the process. If he was going to be caught, he certainly was not going to come quietly.

Having clearly shown that he was an extremely dangerous individual to both police and public alike, a manhunt was underway to capture Martin as soon as possible, for everybody's safety. Part of the police operation included placing Martin's girlfriend and her home under surveillance, and this eventually proved fruitful as Martin, dressed as a woman, turned up at her flat only to be confronted by the police. A struggle ensued during his arrest and he produced a gun, which resulted in one of the officers shooting him. Unperturbed, Martin continued the struggle and pulled out another gun, before being overpowered without any further shots being fired by either him or the police.

After having had his wounds treated, Martin was eventually released into police custody, when he then had to attend Marlborough Street Magistrates' Court charged with a list of various offences, including attempted murder. His appearance at court continued for several days, each of which required him to be brought back and forth from Brixton prison, where he was being held on remand. On 24 December 1982, whilst waiting in the cells for his appearance in court, he somehow managed to escape, prompting another massive police manhunt in an effort to recapture him. It was Martin's escape which would ultimately lead to the police shooting of Stephen Waldorf some two weeks later.

On the day of the shooting, the police, who had Martin's girlfriend, Sue Stephens, under surveillance, followed her as she travelled as a backseat passenger in a yellow Mini, and whose front-seat passenger, Stephen Waldorf, somewhat resembled Martin. The car was being driven by a third, unidentified, man, when the car came to a stop in traffic. Detective Constable Finch of the Metropolitan Police, who was armed and in an unmarked car following Stephens, was the only officer at the scene who had actually met Martin and knew what he looked like. As Finch got out of his vehicle and approached the Mini on the nearside to confirm that the front seat passenger was in fact Martin, the passenger in the front reached onto the back seat, which Finch misinterpreted as someone reaching for a gun. In the heat of the moment and with adrenalin pulsing around his body, DC Finch drew his handgun and opened fire, initially aiming at the Mini's tyres, before aiming at the front-seat passenger. This resulted in total confusion amongst his colleagues, with one of them, Detective Constable Deane, opening fire through the vehicle's rear window because he was under the misapprehension that Finch was being fired on from somebody in the car. Another colleague, Detective Constable Jardine, also opened fire. Despite the fact that a number of their shots had clearly hit the passenger, and with Finch having run out of ammunition, he decided to strike him with his firearm. It was only after this that the three officers realised that the man they had just shot was not David Martin, but Stephen Waldorf.

Collectively, the men had fired fourteen rounds into the car, but despite the officers' close proximity to it, only five of them actually struck Waldorf. It was sheer luck that none of the other eight rounds had hit Sue Stephens, although she was grazed by one of them. Waldorf also sustained a fractured skull. In the aftermath of the incident, both Detective Constable Finch and Detective Constable Jardine were charged with the attempted murder of Stephen Waldorf, along with grievous bodily harm, but both men were acquitted at court in October 1983. Waldorf survived and was paid compensation by the Metropolitan Police, and Martin was eventually arrested on 28 January 1983 by members of the Metropolitan Police's Flying Squad in an underground tunnel between Hampstead and Belsize Park tube stations. He stood trial at the Old Bailey in September of the same year, charged with fourteen offences, one of which was the attempted murder of a police officer. Having been found guilty of all charges, he was sentenced to twenty-five years' imprisonment but committed suicide in his prison cell in March 1984.

The investigation into the shooting of Waldorf received nationwide public attention. Having been extensively reported in the press, it was even debated in parliament, with the major concern being the potential danger to members of the public of having armed police officers. It was clear to most right-minded thinking people that the shooting of Stephen Waldorf was wrong on so many levels, and that the police use of firearms needed to be tightened up dramatically, both from the actual firearms aspect, as well as tactically. The description of what happened in the shooting sounded more like something out of a Wild West shootout than it did a well-planned police firearms operation.

This was also quite possibly the first occasion when large numbers of fellow firearms officers handed in their police firearms permits in protest at the decision to prosecute their colleagues. It is also possible that some of them took this decision so as not to find themselves in such a position in the future.

The Waldorf case once again highlighted the perils faced by firearms officers in such situations and the possibility that they could end up being charged with murder for doing their job, or if they got it wrong having made a genuine mistake.

The shooting of Stephen Waldorf resulted in a major turning point in relation to the police use of firearms and how and when they were issued and used. At the time it caused such a shock, not only in the eyes of politicians, but members of the public as well.

Home Secretary William Whitelaw commissioned a report entitled 'Guidelines on the Issue and Use of Firearms by Police', which was sent out to all police forces throughout England and Wales, as it was clear that there had to be a major shift in the mindset when it came to the police and their use of firearms. Two of the points in Whitelaw's guidelines included raising the rank of those who were able to authorise the issuing of firearms, and an emphasis on all officers who were authorised to carry firearms about their own personal responsibilities, which in essence meant that officers were not to pull the trigger of their firearm unless they really had to.

Whitelaw also put together a working group to look closely at all aspects of the police use of firearms. The chair of the group was Geoffrey Dear, who at the time was an assistant Commissioner in the Metropolitan Police. One of the group's remits was not only to look closely at the training officers who were selected to carry firearms within the police, but to look at the officer's individual temperaments and personalities before they were even allowed to undergo the training. The working group published its conclusions and recommendations in what was referred to as the Dear Report, and much of what it included could be described as basic common sense. Improve the training and increase the frequency of the follow-up training to ensure that an officer was still up to the required standard to continue to be authorised to carry firearms for police-related purposes.

The report uniformed the terminology in relation to police firearms officers, creating the term 'Authorised Firearms Officer', and resulted in the publication of the first ever *Manual of Guidance on Police Use of Firearms*.

Although the Waldorf shooting was a turning point in relation to how the police looked at and conducted firearms operations, the learning process was not fast in coming, as was shown with the shootings of Cherry Groce as well as 5-year-old John Shorthouse by police in 1985. These incidents led to a further working group being set up in 1986 by the Home Office, with the two main recommendations coming from its subsequent report being an emphasis on having fewer firearms officers and that those remaining would become part of a specialist, dedicated and smaller armed unit. The other suggestion was the establishment of what the report referred to as roving armed patrols, which would later become known as Armed Response Vehicles (ARVs).

CHAPTER NINETEEN

The Shooting of PC Brian 'Bill' Bishop, 1984

On 22 August 1984 PC Brian 'Bill' Bishop of Essex Police was shot in the head whilst on a firearms operation in Frinton-on-Sea. He died five days later in St Bartholomew's Hospital in London, having never regained consciousness.

In the lead up to the operation, a team of officers from the FSU had been looking to arrest a man who had already carried out two armed robberies in the Walton and Frinton area.

The following information about Bill comes from his wife, Sue Bishop. In 1997 she wrote an article about him for the Essex Police History notebook series. The following are excerpts taken from it.

Brian Bishop was born on 24 July 1947 and joined the former Essex Constabulary as a fifteen-year-old Cadet. Whilst a cadet, the Dog Handlers gave him the nickname, 'Bill'. This was due to his hair. A bit thin on top but long and wavy at the back, which reminded them of the famous American cowboy from the late nineteenth century, Wild Bill Hickock.

Brian was attested as Police Constable 389 on 11 August 1966 and was posted to Colchester. Two years later he joined the dog section as a handler. In 1975 he joined the Force Support Unit and subsequently became a firearms instructor. At six feet seven inches tall he was known as a gentle giant.

On Wednesday, 22 August 1984, along with other members of the FSU, he was called to Central Avenue in Frinton, a short distance from the sea front. This call followed on from reports that earlier in the day a man had robbed two post offices, one in Frinton and the other in nearby Walton. It was also known that he had hidden his haul of several thousand pounds alongside a railway embankment.

The wanted man had held up the post office staff with a sawn-off shotgun and had forced them to hand over money before escaping on a motorcycle.

Following the first raid, he had been stopped and questioned by Police as he fitted the description of the wanted man. He was then taken to his mother's house as she was living nearby. She gave him an alibi and said that he had been at home all afternoon. He was then released to commit the second raid.

Meanwhile, Police had kept watch on the site where the cash had been hidden. Finally, the robber approached carrying what appeared to be a carrier bag. Constable Bishop shouted at him, 'Armed Police, stop!' at which point the robber lifted the carrier bag, which concealed a gun, and shot him in the head. Sergeant (later Inspector) Mervyn Fairweather was shot in the groin. Another colleague then fired at the gunman, hitting him in the back and side.

Constable Bishop died five days later at Saint Bartholomew's Hospital in London.

A thirty-five-year-old man from Brentwood was arrested at the scene, but because of the injuries he'd sustained, he was detained under armed guard at Colchester Hospital.

On Friday, 19 July 1985 he appeared at Norwich Crown Court sitting in a wheelchair as he was paralysed from the waist down. He was charged with Constable Bishop's murder and the attempted murder of

Sergeant Fairweather. He denied both charges. The jury subsequently found him guilty of Brain Bishop's murder, but remarkably they found him not guilty of attempting to murder Sergeant Fairweather, but guilty of wounding him. He was sentenced to life imprisonment and the Judge commented that he would recommend a minimum of twenty years in prison had his injuries not reduced his danger to society.

Mr Justice Boreham, the Judge in the case, also praised the bravery of the officers who had been with Brian Bishop when confronted by the robber and went on to say, 'I only wish Constable Bishop was here to hear the commendation.'

On Wednesday, 19 February 1986, the then Home Secretary, Douglas Hurd, unveiled a brown granite memorial stone adjacent to the seafront site where Brian fell. It was funded by the Police Memorial Trust, set up in 1984 following the death of WPC Yvonne Fletcher in St James Square, London, and was the brainchild of film director, Michael Winner. The aim of the trust is to erect memorials to Police officers killed in the course of their hazardous duty, on the spot where they met their death, thereby acting as a permanent reminder to the public they serve, of their sacrifice.

Brian Bishop's memorial was only the third to be funded by the trust and the first outside of London.

A guard of honour was provided by colleagues from the Force Support Unit and despite snow flurries and a chilling wind, several hundred members of the public attended the unveiling ceremony. In attendance with me, his widow Sue, a former Policewoman, was our son David and Brian's parents. We laid floral tributes. Mr Hurd laid a spray of flowers.

As the ceremony came to a close, Sergeant Fairweather marched alone to the memorial, saluted and marched off, a fitting tribute from a man injured when his colleague received fatal injuries.

A small wrought iron fence has since been erected around the memorial by the local council and a garden dug inside. School children *have planted spring bulbs along the green beside it. In Walton-on-the-Naze, the Council have named a road on a new housing estate, 'Brian Bishop Close'.*

When I began my Essex Police career back in the summer of 1983, I got to know Sue when I started playing football for the force. At the time she was heavily involved with the football section, even down to looking after my elder son, Luke, who was about 3 at the time, who used to come along to watch me play at most of our home games.

It was whilst playing football for Essex Police that I decided I wanted to become a member of the FSU. At the time the late John Rhymes, who had been one of the unit's original Sergeants, was the manager of the football team and his assistant was Charlie Clark, who later went on to become a Deputy Chief Constable. Also in the team way back then were Phil O'Connell, Roy Scanes, John Weatherly, Cliff Haines and John 'Kiltsy' Stewart, all of whom were unit members at the time. Some of their stories, coupled with the obvious camaraderie they shared, made up my mind about which direction I wanted my police career to go in.

It took me another six years to eventually get there, but finally, in September 1989, I achieved my goal when I became a fully-fledged member of the FSU.

Brian 'Bill' Bishop remains the last member of Essex Police to be killed on duty whilst trying to safeguard members of our community.

When I spoke with Sue Bishop about her husband's killing, it was clear to me when speaking with her the depth of love she still had for Bill. We discussed which photograph of Bill she would like to see in the book. Straight away she chose what I believe is an almost iconic image, taken at Stansted Airport on 5 June 1983, when the American space shuttle *Enterprise* stopped off in the UK on its way back home from that year's Paris air show.

I also spoke to Inspector Merv Fairweather, who was a Sergeant at the time of the shooting, although he is retired now, and who was alongside Bill at Frinton and was wounded in the same incident. Merv typed up his recollection of the events of that day, and what took place in the immediate aftermath. What follows is his personal account.

During the afternoon of Wednesday, 22 August 1984 two armed robberies occurred at post offices within the Coastal areas of North Essex:

At 4:25pm at Walton post office, a male wearing a stocking mask produced a sawn-off shotgun, threatened staff and made off with about £9,000.

At 4:40pm the same individual attempted to rob Frinton post office but left empty handed after threatening staff and customers with the shotgun. On leaving the scene of this robbery, he was chased by a 19-year-old travel clerk, who wisely gave up the chase when he was threatened with the shotgun.

He left both scenes on a high-powered motorcycle.

Following the report a short time later from a member of the public, that a motorcyclist had deposited what was thought to be rubbish in a wooded area of Central Avenue, Frinton, police attended that location and discovered a large amount of bank notes in a plastic bag within Pedlars Wood. The cash was substituted with newspaper and an OP (Observation Point) was set up on the site of the 'find' (this was manned by local unarmed CID officers).

About 8:15pm a team of nine armed officers, including Bill and I, from the Tactical Firearms Group arrived and placed armed containment each end of Central Avenue. Once this was in place, the unarmed OP was withdrawn.

About 8:30pm a motorcycle was parked at the seaward end of Central Avenue, close to the plain police car containing four of the armed officers (including Bill and myself). The rider, whom I now know to be Colin Richards, dismounted from the bike, removed his helmet and took a black plastic bag from the rear carrier of the motorcycle.

He then made his way along Central Avenue towards the wooded area carrying the plastic bag.

The police team that was located at the other end of Central Avenue (towards Walton Road) saw the motorcyclist enter, leave the wood and walk around the area over a number of minutes. It would be fair to say that at this time and location radio communication was poor between the two elements of the police firearms team. It was felt necessary to relocate our vehicle in order to obtain an update on the situation and tighten the containment. In the process of manoeuvring the vehicle, we were confronted by the motorcyclist (Richards) returning toward his machine along Central Avenue. At this stage he did not appear to recognise us as police officers.

Our driver drove straight past Richards and stopped at an angle to his rear. Bill was getting out of the vehicle as we stopped and immediately began to follow Richards. To the best of my knowledge, I was the next person out of the vehicle (I was seated in the rear nearside passenger seat behind Bill).

Bill was, by this time between Richards and me. I moved out and to my left to assist Bill, who had now drawn his revolver and begun to challenge Richards with words to the effect of 'Stop! Armed police.' Richards ignored the initial challenge and kept on walking toward the motorcycle. Bill repeated his request. Richards then turned, lowered his body into a half crouch and discharged what I now know to be a sawn-off double-barrelled side-by-side shotgun in our direction (which had been hidden inside the plastic bag). I can recall seeing the flash and pieces of the plastic bag fly out from the middle of his body. I felt a violent impact in the area of my groin that spun me to my left. As I righted myself, I saw Bill slowly collapsing to the ground and Richards was moving away to my right, apparently operating the mechanism of his firearm. (I can only recall hearing one shot from his weapon.) I feared he was in the process of reloading and therefore my life and that of other officers was under immediate threat. I therefore fired one shot in the direction of Richards from my .38 revolver. Richards ceased his actions with his firearm, straightened up, went forward a couple of paces and collapsed.

I made my way as fast as I could to a cover position, where I joined another officer from our team. We were near to where Richards lay, and we challenged him to release his hold on the shotgun, which he failed to do.

Within a few seconds another officer gained a superior cover position behind a nearby parked car and took over the challenge. At this officer's request, which went along the lines of, 'Bill's bad, Merv, get an ambulance,' I crawled back to the police vehicle and radioed for an ambulance and further assistance. As I recall, the personal radios were ineffective.

Whilst making my way to the vehicle, I heard further challenges being shouted by my colleague. Within a few minutes the other team of four officers arrived at the scene and Richards was disarmed and detained. We gave Bill what first aid we could, but I could see that he was gravely injured.

Between attempting to assist with Bill and my collection by ambulance, I lay on the road with my feet elevated into the car. Both Bill and Richards were evacuated in separate ambulances within a short space of time. I was not removed from the scene until about 9:10pm. In retrospect, I have no doubt this was the right decision as I was the least seriously injured. All three of us were taken to the Essex County Hospital in Colchester, where we were detained.

Tragically, Bill died five days later. I underwent surgery to remove the shot from my groin, but due to the location (close to the femoral artery), it remains in place to this day.

Richards remained at the Essex County Hospital, under guard, for some considerable time. He was partially paralysed as a result of his injuries and, to the best of my knowledge, remains wheelchair bound to this day.

I remained in hospital for over a week, during which time, amongst other well wishes, I received two letters from prison. As these were from previous 'clients' of mine (individuals whom I had arrested), I found them particularly moving.

I was released from hospital in time to attend Bill's funeral, which I did in uniform. Following some weeks convalescing at home, I returned to full operational duties as a patrol Sergeant at Colchester and resumed as a member of the TFG some months later.

I became aware of the following facts whilst awaiting the matter being brought to trial:

- *Between the robberies and the murder, Richards had been stopped by police but alibied by his mother.*
- *Both the other officers with Bill and I had discharged our weapons, but I was only aware of Richards shooting and me shooting my weapon. (This is probably down to perceptual distortion, something I feel we sometimes forget when dealing with victims and witnesses.)*
- *I was surprised to learn that it was felt that I had missed with my shot. It was not a 'reaction' but a fast aimed shot for the reasons given. I can recall registering that I had a safe 'backstop' and as stated above, I did not hear or see anyone else's actions, but saw a reaction from Richards, following my shot.*
- *Richards was using 'large game shot' in his shotgun. The piece I have lodged in my groin is about the size of a .22.*
- *Richards was in fact known as 'Solo', the subject sought by us for a number of armed robberies in Essex and the Met.*
- *Richards had previously discharged a firearm at a Met. Police motorcyclist following a previous robbery at Lloyds Bank, Romford, on 1 March 1983.*

Richards was convicted the following year at Norwich Crown Court for Bill's murder, GBH with intent on me, and a number of robberies including those outlined above. He received a life sentence.

The period of the trial was particularly difficult for a number of reasons. Any crown court appearance can be a little stressful but, on this occasion, my colleagues and I had to recount in detail the facts leading up to and throughout the murder of a friend and colleague, whilst suffering the obvious rigorous cross examination by an eminent QC.

At the end of the trial, the judge commended the officers involved in which he made a particularly fitting tribute to Bill.

My feelings looking back now over all these years are probably best summed up by the fact that the pain of my injury and subsequent treatment are virtually forgotten within a short period of time, however the pain of losing a colleague and friend under the circumstances described remains today and will, undoubtedly, for the rest of my days.

The then Chief Constable of Essex, Sir Robert Bunyard, said at Bill's funeral that he was all that was best in a British police officer. Those words would undoubtably be endorsed by all that knew him.

I met Merv Fairweather at Essex Police HQ in Chelmsford in 2012 and spoke with him about the shooting at Frinton. Merv is a very humble individual and a wonderful human being. He retired in 1995, having reached the heady heights of the rank of Inspector, with his later years being spent mainly working at the force training school at headquarters Chelmsford. He remains to this day a true gent.

During the incident at Frinton, Merv was shot at the same time as Bill, and although he was immediately aware he had been hit by the gunman, he did not tell any of his colleagues and simply carried on following what his training had taught him to do. It was only after about ten minutes, when he had an adrenalin dump and physically could not carry on, that his colleagues were aware that he had also been hit by the gunman.

Merv returned to work about six weeks after the shooting and decided that he would continue as a firearms officer, with the support of both his family and colleagues. He regained his police firearms permit less than a year later, before the trial of the gunman who had shot him and sadly taken Bill's life.

The following are the words of the then Chief Constable of Essex Police, Roger S. Bunyard, which appeared in the September/October 1984 issue of Essex Police's newspaper, *The Law*.

OBITUARY

TO RECORD the death of a colleague in any circumstances is always a sad task. To have to announce the deaths of two officers of this force in such a short space of time, and under such terrible circumstances is a tragedy.

Legal restraints limit the comments that I can make about the circumstances which led to each death, and I must restrict myself to assuring the families of both officers that the entire force shares their grief. We extend to them our deepest sympathy and offer our heartfelt support in their time of need.

Of the officers themselves, I can only say that both were respected as men of stature. One was a seasoned officer, well versed in police matters, the other a probationary constable at the threshold of a new career, but both will be remembered for their many fine qualities and for their comradeship. They will be sadly missed.

The epitaph next to Bishop's memorial stone on Frinton sea front, close to where he was shot, summarises the circumstances surrounding his death as follows.

Brian Bishop, a member of the Essex Police Tactical Firearms Group was called here to await the return of an armed robber to collect stolen money which he had hidden following post office raids in Walton and Frinton. Brian challenged the suspect who immediately opened fire causing extensive head injuries from which Brian subsequently died. A man was convicted of his murder.

'Bill' went out to work one day and said goodbye to his family. His job was to help keep the people of Essex safe, and in doing so, he paid with his life.

CHAPTER TWENTY

The Shooting of Cherry Groce, 1985

Four years before Cherry Groce was shot, the Brixton riots of 1981 had taken place due to a breakdown of the relationship between the local community and the Metropolitan Police. The large African-Caribbean population of Brixton had felt that the officers who policed the areas they lived in were racist, and that this belief was born out by the treatment they received from them. This meant that there was a constant tension between the two factions, which was never far from boiling point.

The shooting of Cherry Groce by police on 28 September 1985 not only led to further Brixton riots, but to subsequent ones that took place in Peckham in south London, Toxteth in Liverpool and the Broadwater Farm estate in Tottenham, north London.

Dorothy 'Cherry' Groce was shot by Detective Chief Inspector Douglas Lovelock, of the Metropolitan Police, after they had gone to her address in Normandy Road, Lambeth, looking for her 21-year-old son, Michael, who was wanted for questioning in relation to a robbery and a suspected firearms offence.

Michael Groce had become involved with local street gangs during his teenage years, and by 1985 had been in trouble with the police on a number of occasions. He had only been released from prison just two months prior to his mother's death.

A few days before the riots in 1985 began, Michael became embroiled in an argument with his girlfriend at his mother's home. He became so angry that he allegedly fired a sawn-off shotgun into a piece of his mother's furniture. Not long after this there was a knock at the front door of the premises. Michael went to see who it was and what they wanted, only to come face to face with a police officer, who asked him if he was Michael Groce. When the officer stopped him from closing the door on him, Michael allegedly pointed the gun in the officer's face in an effort to get him to back off so that he could close the door. The officer, and his colleagues who were with him, were from Hertfordshire Constabulary, who had not informed the Metropolitan Police that they were coming on to their 'Manor' to try to arrest Michael Groce. Once the Metropolitan Police became aware of the situation, they determined that Groce was an armed, violent and dangerous individual, which resulted in the officers who were searching for him being armed.

On the morning of Saturday, 28 September 1985, believing that Michael Groce was at his mother's home, police forced their way into the house looking for him, believing that he could be armed. This was in relation to an armed robbery which had taken place at a jeweller's shop in Royston, Hertfordshire on 10 September. During the raid, Mrs Groce, who had been asleep in the downstairs front room, heard a noise coming from the hallway. She got out of bed to investigate the noise, believing there might have been intruders in her home. As she got to the closed door, it suddenly flew open towards her and she was confronted by a man aiming a gun at her. Mrs Groce tried to run past him and out of the room, but the officer discharged his weapon and she was shot in the chest and fell to the floor. An ambulance was called so she could receive treatment and be taken to St. Thomas' Hospital in London. In the meantime, news about the raid had spread throughout the community, but unfortunately the facts of what had actually happened had become distorted, to the extent that it was believed Mrs Groce had actually been killed, which she had not.

Having arrived at the hospital, Mrs Groce was operated on and doctors found that the bullet had penetrated her lung and exited her body via her spine, leaving her paralysed from the waist down. She remained in hospital for a year, after which she required rehabilitation for a further twelve months, meaning that those children who were still living with her at the time had to be looked after by family friends. Mrs Groce remained permanently paralysed and needed to use a wheelchair.

Michael Groce handed himself into police a few days after his mother had been shot and was subsequently interviewed in relation to the Hertfordshire armed robbery. Although he was charged with possession of a sawn-off shotgun, for which he faced trial, was found guilty and sentenced to a three-year suspended sentence, he was never charged with the armed robbery in Hertfordshire.

Mrs Groce was paid more than £500,000 in compensation from the Metropolitan Police, but they did not admit any liability for what had happened. The officer who shot Mrs Groce, Douglas Lovelock, was charged and acquitted of maliciously wounding her. Lovelock appeared at the Old Bailey on Thursday, 8 January 1987 to stand trial. He told the court of his tension and fear when leading the raid on Mrs Groce's home, because of his misbelief that Michael Groce had fired a sawn-off shotgun at police.

According to an article in *The Scotsman* newspaper of Friday, 9 January 1987, it came out in court that Lovelock had told the Assistant Chief Constable of West Yorkshire, Mr John Domaille, who had been sent to London to investigate the shooting of Mrs Groce, that he had felt, 'excitement, fear, tension and apprehension' before the raid on Mrs Groce's home, and that his subsequent shooting of her was a 'purely reflex action' and that he had 'no intention whatsoever' of firing his gun. 'This was a complete accident, a terrible, terrible accident. I truly, truly regret it. I saw a flash, I was dumfounded. I thought; "Jesus Christ, this is the end".'

It was not until twenty-nine years later, in March 2014, that the then Commissioner of the Metropolitan Police, Sir Bernard Hogan-Howe, apologised unreservedly to the family of Cherry Groce for the failings of the Metropolitan Police.

The shooting of Cherry Groce directly led to the Metropolitan Police carrying out a review of its entire firearms procedures, which in turn led to only centrally controlled, specialist firearms units being armed and allowed to carry out firearms operations.

The shooting of Cherry Groce highlighted the importance and need for police forces across the country to have a dedicated, full-time and well-trained firearms section as part of their force.

CHAPTER TWENTY-ONE

The Hungerford Massacre, 1987

On Wednesday, 19 August 1987, the counties of Wiltshire and Berkshire were devastated by what became known as the Hungerford Massacre, which resulted in the murders of sixteen people, including an unarmed police officer, Constable Roger Brereton, who was initially shot with a Beretta 9-mm handgun and finished off with a Kalashnikov 7.62-mm semi-automatic rifle.

These murders brought in to being a major transformation in British firearms legislation, the Firearms (Amendment) Act 1988, the most prominent changes being the banning of all handguns, semi-automatic centre-fire rifles, and the restriction on shotguns with a capacity of more than three cartridges, for use by the general public.

The killer in this case, 27-year-old Michael Robert Ryan, who lived at 4 South View, Hungerford with his 63-year-old mother, was described by those who knew him as being somewhat of a loner, and somebody who had no known friends. He had never been arrested nor had a criminal record, and so there were no red flags when he applied for and was allowed to purchase a total of seven firearms, an arsenal which included two shotguns, a Kalashnikov semi-automatic rifle, and a Beretta 9-mm handgun. The weapons had been bought in an eight-month period between 17 December 1986 and 8 August 1987, the latter date being just eleven days before Ryan went on his murderous rampage. Looking back on it now, it is quite remarkable to think that one man was allowed to buy so many lethal weapons in such a short period of time, especially a Kalashnikov rifle, which most people would more than likely associate with being a weapon of choice issued to soldiers from countries throughout Eastern Europe and beyond.

Hungerford is a quiet, picturesque, market town set in the Kennet Valley between Newbury and Marlborough in the Berkshire countryside. The last time there had been a murder in the town was just before Christmas 1876, when Police Inspector Drewcott and Police Constable Shorter, who were both married men with families, were murdered by the poachers William Day, William Tidbury, Francis Tidbury and Henry Tidbury.

The first of Michael Ryan's victims is believed to have been mother of two Mrs Susan Godfrey, who was picnicking in the privately owned Savernake Forest some 7 miles to the west of Hungerford with her two children at about 12:30pm, when she was abducted by Ryan. Her body was later found having been shot thirteen times in the back. It is believed he used the Beretta handgun for this killing. The fact Ryan shot Mrs Godfrey so many times suggests that it was a frenzied attack, and possibly whilst she was trying to run away.

After leaving Savernake Forest, Ryan drove off in his silver Vauxhall Astra towards Hungerford and stopped off enroute at a petrol station to fill up his car and a petrol can with fuel. Without any warning, he opened fire on the female cashier but fortunately for her, the bullet, although having passed through the kiosk's front window, did not hit her. Intent on killing her, Ryan entered the kiosk and aimed his gun at the women, who by now had taken cover beneath the counter, but it failed to go off. Consequently, Ryan got into his car and drove off, continuing his journey towards Hungerford. This particular incident resulted in two calls to the emergency services, one by the cashier and another by a customer who had left the petrol station just after Ryan arrived.

These first two incidents inadvertently caused much confusion, because the reports had gone to two different police forces. Thames Valley Police sent officers to the petrol station, whilst it was Wiltshire Police who dispatched officers to Savernake Forest. Despite what had happened at each location, unarmed officers had been sent to both scenes, even though the cashier at the petrol station would have clearly informed the call-taker that she had been shot at. Neither force knew about what the other force was dealing with, so at this stage they were being treated as two totally separate and unrelated incidents.

Ryan arrived back at his home in Hungerford at approximately 12:45pm and then went about dousing it in the petrol he had stolen from the nearby service station. It is known that when he left his home his car would not start, and in a fit of pique, he fired a number of shots at it, before making off on foot (having donned a bullet proof vest), taking with him his two rifles and the Beretta handgun, leaving his three shotguns at home. Before leaving the house, he shot dead his two dogs.

Ryan went to the house of his neighbours, Mr and Mrs Mason, at 6 South View, and shot both dead. Mr Mason with the Kalashnikov, and Mrs Mason with his handgun. The time of these two killings was sometime before 1pm. After shooting the Masons, Ryan made off on foot and started making his way to the local common. Enroute, he shot and wounded two women. First was teenage schoolgirl Lisa Mildenhall, who had heard the shootings and gone to see what all the commotion was about. Ryan shot her four times in the legs but left her where she fell and did not attempt to finish her off. If his shots were aimed, then Ryan clearly had no intention of killing her. Despite her injuries, she survived.

Mrs Marjorie Jackson, who had seen Ryan return home, was shot in the back by him, but after he had shot her, he moved on without checking to see if she was alive or dead. Thankfully, she survived. Possibly because she was in a state of shock, Mrs Jackson telephoned a friend of her husband's rather than the police or ambulance.

By just after 1pm the police had received several calls and had made the connection between the shooting at the petrol station and those that were taking place in Hungerford.

A Mr Kenneth Clements was the next to be killed as he walked with family members and their dog along a footpath that connected South View with the common. Despite being with others, it was only Mr Clements who was shot. The others managed to escape the area before Ryan could make his mind up as to whether he was going to shoot them or not.

Ryan walked back down the footpath and into South View and headed in the general direction of his home. By now PC Roger Brereton, who was single crewed, and, more importantly, was unarmed, had been dispatched due to the number of phone calls reporting shots being fired in South View. Another unit had also been dispatched and between the two, they decided that their best option was to try to contain the street. The Thames Valley firearms unit had still not been deployed to the area.

Caught unawares, PC Brereton was sat in his patrol vehicle when Ryan shot him through the windscreen of his car, striking him in the chest. Despite his wounds, PC Brereton was able to make a call on his radio stating he had been shot and also confirming they were dealing with an armed individual, just before Ryan finished him off with a burst from his Kalashnikov rifle. Not long before PC Brereton was shot, the controller in the force control room had issued a clear and precise warning to all police patrols in Hungerford that the person they were looking for may well be in possession of firearms, and that they were to exercise maximum care.

No sooner had Ryan murdered PC Brereton, than a car with Mrs Linda Chapman and her daughter, Alison, in it pulled into

South View. Ryan wasted no time in opening fire, hitting both of them. Despite her injuries, Mrs Chapman was able to put the car into reverse and drive out of South View before Ryan could fire at them again.

Several events then took place in quick succession. Ryan's next victim was 84-year-old Mr Abdur Khan, who was shot dead whilst he was in the back garden of his house at 24 Fairview Road, and not long after that he shot and wounded a Mr Alan Lepetit, also in Fairview Road.

Despite no police firearms officers having been deployed to the scene, an ambulance arrived and reversed into South View. As it came into Ryan's view, he opened fire and one of the crew, Hazel Haslett, was slightly injured. Without any further ado, the ambulance drove off just as quickly as it had arrived.

Two police officers who had arrived in South View came across the son of Mr Clements at the east end of the street, who told them where he had last seen the shooter. Despite not being armed, the officers, along with young master Clements, made their way back along the road before running into Ryan, who fired upon them. By sheer luck, none of them was hit. Shortly after this, at just after 1:10pm, one of the two officers, believed to have been traffic officer Police Constable Jeremy Wood, made a call on his radio, specifically requesting that the Tactical Firearms Unit (TFU) of Thames Valley Police be deployed to Hungerford. Unfortunately, the unit was taking part in a training exercise some 40 miles away in Otmoor, Oxfordshire, meaning it would be nearly an hour before they would arrive at Hungerford.

PC Woods had taken it upon himself to set up a command post on Hungerford Common, some 500 yards away from where he had last seen Ryan on South View.

Soon afterwards a car containing Mrs Jackson's husband, Ivor, and his friend and colleague Mr George White, who Mrs Jackson had phoned after she had been shot, drove into South View. Ryan immediately opened fire, killing Mr White instantly and wounding Mr Jackson, who pretended to be dead in the hope that Ryan would not shoot him again. His ploy worked.

The next person Ryan killed was his own mother, Dorothy. She had been out shopping when he had originally returned home. She got out of her vehicle and despite seeing the bullet-laden vehicles, blood and the dead bodies, she approached her son, one can only surmise to either remonstrate or reason with him. Despite being his mother, he turned his gun on her, shooting her four times, before calmly walking off. By now, Ryan had shot sixteen people, seven of whom he had killed. Police officers were sent to deal with the large number of reported shootings, but not one of them had a firearm.

After shooting and killing his mother, Ryan walked back along South View and left it via a footpath at the east end of the street, before making his way across the local playing fields. It was there he shot and wounded Mrs Betty Tolladay, who was in the front garden of her home in Clarks Gardens, and who had shouted at him to 'kindly stop that racket'. Without an apparent care in the world, Ryan continued on his way and soon reached the War Memorial Recreation Grounds.

It was just before 1:20pm, some fifty minutes after Ryan had murdered his first victim, that PC Wood was joined by two armed colleagues at the makeshift command post he had set up on the common.

Having reached the recreation grounds, Ryan came across the innocent and unsuspecting Mr Francis Butler, who was out walking his dog. Sadly for Mr Butler, he was in the wrong place at the wrong time and Ryan shot him dead. After leaving the recreation grounds, Ryan's next victim was local taxi driver Mr Marcus Barnard, who was shot dead whilst driving along the road.

As Ryan reached the junction of Bulpit Lane and Priory Avenue, he fired at a car that was being driven along the latter of the two roads by Mrs Ann Honeybone. Although wounded, she managed to drive off and survived the attack. Once again Ryan simply walked off along the road and when he reached the junction with Hillside Road, he came across Mr John Storms, who was sat in his car. Without any warning, he shot him. Although badly wounded, Mr Storms survived.

A short while later, a car driven by Mr Douglas Wainwright, who was with his wife, Kathleen, innocently pulled up alongside Ryan in Fairview Road, not knowing who he was or what he had been doing. Ryan fired into the vehicle, killing Mr Wainwright and wounding Mrs Wainwright. The couple were only in the town to visit their son, Trevor, who was a police officer stationed in Hungerford. Whilst in the same street he shot and wounded Mr Kevin Lance, who just happened to be driving along the road in his Ford Transit van. Not long afterwards, at the junction of Tarrants Hill and Priory Avenue, Ryan came across another Transit van, this time being driven by Mr Eric Vardy, who was shot and killed.

Although several of the individuals who Ryan shot had been driving, at no time did he try to get into any of the vehicles and drive away from the area, suggesting that however he saw his day eventually coming to an end, it was always going to be in Hungerford.

Ryan's next victim was Sandra Hill, who he shot and killed whilst she was driving her Renault in Priory Road. He kept on walking along the road, when for no known reason he forced his way into number 60 Priory Road, which was the home of Mr and Mrs Gibbs. He shot both, killing Mr Gibbs instantly. Mrs Gibbs survived initially but subsequently died of her injuries in hospital. After leaving the Gibbs' home, Ryan fired blindly at two houses on the opposite side of the road, injuring two persons in the process. Mr Michael Jennings at 62 Priory Road, and Mrs Myra Geater from number 71.

A short while later, the last person to receive what were to be fatal injuries was shot further along Priory Road. The victim was

Mr Ian Playle. He was struck by a single shot fired from Ryan's Beretta handgun and died of his injuries two days later.

The last person shot by Ryan was Mr George Moon, who was in the back porch of his home at 109 Priory Road when Ryan shot him. Thankfully, Mr Moon survived. The time now was 1:45pm, an hour and fifteen matters after Ryan had murdered his first victim. The last sighting of Ryan was soon after the last of his shootings, when he was seen near to the rear of the town's John O'Gaunt School.

Although many of those who had been killed or wounded would have known each other, their shootings had no obvious connection to Ryan; he had not been at school with or worked with any of them. They were just innocent people who he had simply come across whilst he wandered around the streets of Hungerford.

With the benefit of hindsight, what did not help the overall situation in its early stages was that the sound of gunshots around Hungerford Common, while a regular occurrence, was not unusual, meaning that initially those who heard the shots, whether in their homes, on foot or in their vehicles, were not necessarily startled or too readily alarmed.

The subsequent report on the Hungerford shootings by Mr Colin Smith, CVO, QPM, the Chief Constable of Thames Valley Police, produced for the Home Secretary Douglas Hurd included several relevant points.

During the ninety-eight minutes between the time of the first emergency call at 12:40pm and the last at 2:18pm, a total of eighty-three calls were received at the Newbury public telephone exchange. This highlights one of the issues of such events, because despite the last of Ryan's victims having been shot at 1:45pm, emergency calls about the shootings were still being received more than half an hour later. Some of these calls included sightings, but as Ryan was constantly moving about, no sooner had the call been received then it was obsolete and unreliable.

The police officers who originally responded to the incident had an unenviable task. First and foremost, none of them was carrying firearms. They then had to attempt to locate the gunman, despite not knowing what he looked like or where he actually was. Whilst trying to do this they also had to deal with wounded individuals and urge members of the public to take cover and stay indoors, which was sound advice. But this was not a static situation, it was a fluid one that was constantly changing, with the police having to operate from the back foot, as they could not adopt an offensive strategy because they were unarmed. During the hour-long incident, it is known that at least four police officers were fired upon, with PC Brereton being among those murdered by Ryan.

The first firearms officer arrived in Hungerford at 1:20pm and was joined eight minutes later by a second. By 2pm, the number of armed officers had risen to seven. By 2:15pm the members of the force's Tactical Firearms Team had arrived, and the total number of armed police officers in Hungerford had risen to forty-eight. Despite having so many firearms officers, there were still limitations as to what these officers could do, as Thames Valley Police did not possess any armoured vehicles at the time. This meant that some of those who were wounded, along with the bodies of those who had been killed, could not be safely reached. This was rectified at 4:10pm when two armoured Land Rovers, which had been requested by Thames Valley Police from the Metropolitan Police, arrived in the town, allowing the last of the wounded members of the public to be collected safely.

By now it was strongly believed that the man police were looking for was holed up in John O'Gaunt School. This was confirmed at just after 5pm when a shot was heard coming from within the school buildings. Members of the police's Tactical Firearms Team moved in to surround and contain the school. A number of shots were subsequently heard, but none of them appeared to have been aimed at the police officers. It is believed that the shots were fired by Ryan at helicopters in the skies over Hungerford, one of which was a police helicopter, while the rest were from different news outlets.

Ryan threw his Kalashnikov out of a window on the third storey of the school buildings just before 5:30pm. A Sergeant from the Tactical Firearms Team started a conversation with him, during which he confirmed who he was, as well as telling the officer that he had a handgun and a hand grenade. At one stage Ryan said to the officer, 'none of this would have happened but for the policeman coming on the scene.' A reference to PC Brereton. But his statement did not make any sense, however, as by the time he shot and killed PC Brereton, he had already murdered three people.

At 6:52pm a single shot rang out from within the school and after that, there was no further conversation between Ryan and the police. Conversations were then had as to the relevance of the shot, and what weapons Ryan may still have had with him. Thanks to the mention of the grenade, considerations also had to be made in relation to the potential of him having set some kind of booby trap for the officers. After much discussion and planning, members of the Tactical Firearms Team entered the school at 8:10pm to find Ryan dead with a gunshot wound to his head.

Several officers suffered with symptoms of stress in the aftermath of the shootings. It was not just firearms officers or the unarmed officers who had dealt with the incident on the ground, however, but control room staff as well. This was of course a time when men in particular very rarely admitted to experiencing such feelings. They simply kept their thoughts to themselves and got on with things.

The inquest into the shootings took place at Hungerford over four days on 24, 25, 28 and 29 September 1987. In his summing up, the coroner for West Berkshire, Mr Charlie Hoile, included the following remarks:

I would think there may be two areas where your minds might well be moving towards, if there is anything you can suggest to prevent similar fatalities. Clearly the response of the police is an important matter, and how quickly that came about. I would like to say this, that was as a nation, or community, cannot have it both ways, by that I mean we cannot insist upon an unarmed police force and at the same time expect that police in an emergency of that sort, to become armed and become available at 'the drop of a hat'. We have got to accept the fact that we have got to pay for the privilege of having a police force which is, if you like, on our side, not threatening us, an important part of our liberty. Most people would be very reluctant to say do away with that.

The other thing that you may be thinking about is the question of firearms and you will remember that this is a matter which has already exercised the mind of the Home Secretary.

The Jury felt that semi-automatic weapons should not generally be available and that an individual should not be allowed to own an unlimited quantity of arms and ammunition. However, knowing that this subject is under review by the Government, the Jury makes no detailed recommendations.

At the time there were a total of 34,188 people in the Thames Valley Police area who held a shotgun certificate, which allowed these individuals to possess an unlimited number of shotguns. As well as this, 6,301 people in the same policing area held firearms certificates, allowing them to own a total of 15,268 firearms, including handguns, rifles and semi-automatic weapons. There were 451 people who owned between six and ten firearms, and ninety-one who owned more than ten. This was clearly something that had to change.

The killings in Hungerford and the surrounding area that took place on 19 August 1987 remain one of the worst tragedies the nation has ever endured. That one day affected so many lives for so many different reasons. For those who lost friends and family members, the aftermath is even more tragic as they do not know, and will never know, why Ryan did what he did on that fateful day.

CHAPTER TWENTY-TWO

The Sudanese Hijacking, 1996

On the evening of Monday, 25 August 1996, Flight 150, a Sudan Airways Airbus 310 carrying 186 passengers and thirteen crew, took off from the Sudanese capital of Khartoum enroute to Amman, Jordan. About twenty-five minutes after the aircraft had taken off, an unidentified man made his way to the cockpit and commandeered the plane and demanded to be flown to the United Kingdom, after claiming to have in his possession a hand grenade and some dynamite.

The aircraft's pilot had originally contacted Cairo airport to request permission to fly through Egyptian air space to Rome, explaining that his aircraft had been hijacked, but after realising he would not have enough fuel to be able to make the journey, he decided his next best option was to make his way to Cyprus, where the aircraft eventually landed at the country's Larnaca International Airport, to refuel. At this time there was little available information about what was happening, other than the fact that the man who spoke with Cypriot authorities disclosed to them that he wanted to seek political asylum in the UK. He provided no information about the number of hijackers on board, or if any of the passengers or crew had been injured or killed. Despite attempts by Cypriot police to try to release some of the passengers as a good will gesture, the hijacker refused. After the aircraft had refuelled, and two hours after it had landed, the decision was taken not to attempt to storm it, but instead to let it take off and make its way to its intended destination, where it would be dealt with. The plane eventually landed at Stansted Airport at 4:30am on the morning of Tuesday, 26 August.

Amongst those already at the airport waiting for the aircraft to arrive, and hopefully bring the incident to a peaceful conclusion, were members of the Essex Police Tactical Firearms Group (TFG), including myself.

What has become known as the Sudanese Hijacking finally came to an end later that day when all the hostages and crew were safely released, and those responsible were arrested.

What follows are my recollections of that momentous day, including an insight into what goes on in the background to ensure the required personnel and equipment are in place to effectively deal with the incident whilst it is live.

It was just gone 1am when the phone rang. Everybody in the household was already in bed asleep. I was woken up by the feel of my wife's elbow connecting with the lower section of my rib cage.

'The phone's ringing,' my wife had said, abruptly, sounding ever so slightly annoyed at having been woken up at such an unearthly hour of the morning. I had finally managed to stir myself on about the fourth ring and was lying there wondering why she wasn't answering it. My exasperation got the better of me after what seemed an eternity, but what in reality was probably only a matter of seconds.

'Well, answer it then,' I'd said, just as abruptly back, mainly because the phone was on her bedside table.

'Look, nobody is going to be phoning me at this time of the morning so it's obviously your work phoning for you, isn't it? Now answer the bloody thing or I'm going to cut it off because it's getting on my nerves.'

Not wanting to admit that she was actually right about it most probably being for me, I'd leaned over her in a very exaggerated way and answered the phone.

'Good morning. Sorry for the late hour. Its HQ information room here. We have a call out for you. Are you able to turn out?'

I told them I was, having received similar such calls during the night about three or four times a month.

'I can tell you that this call out is in relation to a hijacking incident. I repeat a hijacking incident.' I had heard the female voice on the other end of the line the first time and I was now suddenly even more wide awake than I was before. It's at times like this that your senses all suddenly kick in to life at exactly the same time. I listened intently to what I was been told, gave a few nods of the head and a few grunts of acknowledgement. Why we instinctively nod at times like that when we are talking to somebody on a telephone who cannot see us, I don't know.

'I'll probably be home by lunchtime after getting called out at this time of day, especially as they're trying hard to cut back on the overtime,' I'd told my wife, not sure whether she was asleep or awake.

Little did I know that this was going to be one of the most exhilarating and exciting working days of my life. Spookily enough, in my nine years on the Force Support Unit, the one type of eventuality that we had never done any form of training for was the boarding of an aircraft. We had engaged in vehicle tactics and even practised storming trains and ships from high-powered speed boats in an attempt at releasing hostages, but not an aircraft.

I had been involved in open ground searches before. Searching every type of building that you can think of, but I had never carried out any form of training that involved storming an aircraft.

I arrived at the FSU office at police headquarters in Chelmsford just before 1:30am. Not too bad for someone who was driving a twelve-year-old battered Ford Escort. I collected all my personal kit from the locker room before signing out a Beretta 92f 9-mm handgun and a Hecker & Koch semi-automatic machine gun from the HQ's armoury and meeting up with the other guys in the office. As well as our weaponry and other personal kit, we took three vehicles with us, including the armoured Land Rover and two personnel carriers.

I remember thinking to myself at the time that this was going to be a bit tasty even if everything went according to plan. Although we had had previous hijacking incidents that had been dealt with at Stansted Airport, nobody else who was on the FSU at that time had ever been involved with a hijacking before. The last one was way back in 1981. There was, however, one guy who was still a part of the Weapons Training Department who had been involved in the previous incident.

By 2:30am the entire team had arrived at Stansted and had started the briefing. Stansted is the nominated airport to deal with hijacking situations that come into UK air space, no matter which airport a hijacker asks to be taken to.

'Gentlemen, thank you very much for your attendance here this morning,' the senior officer who was giving the briefing said. 'Sixteen, sorry, make that seventeen, hours ago, a Sudan Airways flight was hijacked soon after it left Khartoum enroute to Amman in the neighbouring country of Jordan. It has since landed once at Larnaca airport in Cyprus, where it was allowed to refuel and then take off again. It is now on its way to the UK and if everything goes according to plan, it's due to land at Stansted at approximately 4am.' The officer conducting the briefing paused to take a sip of his tea.

'What do we know about the hijackers?' he asked rhetorically. 'Well, I can tell you that as best we know, there are seven of them on board the aircraft. Why have they hijacked the plane? The seven hijackers are all believed to be Iraqi military personnel who are in Sudan as military advisors to the Sudanese Army. They have been recalled to Iraq on the orders of Saddam Hussein and the last time Iraqi military personnel were recalled to Iraq from the Sudan, they were shot on their return home.

'It is believed that these guys fear a similar fate awaits them and they have simply chosen to take this course of action to save their own lives. So far, we have had no reports of any of the hostages being hurt or killed and no such threats have been made by the hijackers,' said he continued, as calmly as it was possible to be in such circumstances. 'Gentlemen, do you have any questions at all?' A few hands from some of the guys in our team went up.

The team, positions and locations were all sorted out and everybody was out on the ground waiting for the aircraft to land by 3am. The aircraft arrived on time, as expected, at exactly 4am.

It was still dark, as was usual for the time of year. There was a slight dampness in the air, although it was not cold, and a half-moon shone brightly through a cloudless sky.

The excitement and anticipation began to rise amongst myself and the rest of the team as the engines of the approaching aircraft could be clearly heard overhead. Normal flights are not allowed to land or take off until 6:30am each day. We eventually received confirmation over the radio that the aircraft had finally landed. We then had to wait whilst it made its way from the landing runway to the designated area set aside to deal with such incidents on the north-west side of the airfield. This area was well away from the public gaze and extremely difficult for the press to gain a natural vantage point with their cameras.

I am not sure what time it was, but negotiations had been going on for some time between the guys in the control tower and the hijackers. They had made no actual threats to kill anybody but simply wanted to hand themselves over to the authorities and claim political asylum for themselves and their families, who were with them on the aircraft. I remember that they went to great lengths to point out that their families had no prior knowledge of or took part in the hijacking. I can quite readily believe the latter part of that statement, but not the first part, taking into account that they had made previous attempts to leave Sudan illegally.

Once their motives had been established, there was then discussion over who was going to come off of the aircraft and in what order. The agreement was originally going to be that the 113 hostages would come off first, followed by the six-man crew, one of whom had been stabbed in the arm, then lastly the seven hijackers. This changed when the latter quickly realised that by waiting until last, would place them all in danger. They figured that if they did this, the SAS would then storm the aircraft and kill them all.

I believe the British government had other plans in mind. Having the opportunity to interrogate seven members of the Iraqi military who potentially had no love for their boss – Saddam Hussein – could prove to be a very useful source of useful information. So, killing them all was the last thing that they would want to happen.

The seven men decided that they would come off after the hostages and leave the six-man crew to come off last. This was agreed and so the long, laborious task of getting everybody off the plane as quickly and safely as possible began.

There are always two immediate problems with this. The first is that you initially have to treat everybody as a suspect until it is proved that they are nothing more than an innocent hostage. With lots of elderly and very young children, this is not always an easy task.

By now the passengers had been on the aircraft for nineteen hours, with little to no food or drink. They most probably had not slept much either. They were scared, wondering whether they were going to be killed by their captors, and now they had landed in a foreign country that most, if any, had not been to before. To cap it all, they were now being taken away at gun point to an uncertain future.

The mental stress and strain that most of these people must have been experiencing does not bare thinking about. In these conditions, people can panic and do some very strange things or act in very strange ways.

The second concern in these circumstances is the potential Stockholm Syndrome, where hostages become emotionally attached to their captors and help them escape. This means that you always have to be on your guard. Luckily for us, we had the easy job as we just had to cover them as they left the plane and walked towards our location, which was about 50 yards to the rear of the aircraft. Once they were past our position, they were the responsibility of those behind us who would take care of them. It was about 9:30am before all the hostages were off of the aircraft. Next it was the turn of the hijackers themselves.

I was reminded of this part of the operation recently when one of my sons found an old VHS video cassette in his bedroom, which turned out to be footage of me and colleagues detaining and searching the seven hijackers. Almost all of them were compliant, but one was very arrogant and I came very close to smashing him in the face with the butt of my MP5 because he would not do as he was told. Although he was intimating that he did not understand English, when I decided to test this by asking him whether he had a very small penis, the aggressive look on his face suggested that he understood what I had said perfectly well. I smiled back and simply instructed him to do as he was told, and he reluctantly lay down on the tarmac.

Once taken away from our position, the men were placed in white, one-piece forensic suits that included shoes, gloves and hoods, before being placed in separate vehicles and driven away.

The next phase of the operation saw us by the foot of the aircraft steps whilst the crew alighted form the plane. The last off was the captain, an older grey-haired man who I would guess was in his late fifties. He had a brief case with him, which he was asked to open at the bottom of the steps. He did so willingly, and in it was $250,000 dollars. I had never seen so much money all together in my entire life.

The reason for the cash was that Sudan and the national airline had a zero-credit rating and so had to pay for their landings and take offs in cash. Assuming that the money was for when they landed and took off from Amman airport in Jordan, I dread to think what any of the major airports around the world would charge.

The incident was over and done with by just after 11:30. It had been a very interesting morning at work. One that I had never seen before and one that I would never see again. By the time the next such incident came around, I was long since gone from the Force Support Unit. It was tiring, emotional, draining, testing and yet made me feel very alive. I can remember, looking back on it now, that I did not sleep for three days afterwards thanks to the adrenalin that was still shooting around my body. When I eventually did get to sleep, I slept like a baby for about fourteen hours.

It is fair to say that the FSU more than played its part that day, yet if you read a copy of *The Law* newspaper, which came out in September 1996, you would not have even known we were there. Everybody was mentioned and congratulated, the negotiators, Special Branch, staff in the force information room and contingency planning, yet for some reason, the FSU was not worth a mention. We were obviously so covert that day that nobody knew we were there, even though we were out on the tarmac for the entire eight hours of the operation.

CHAPTER TWENTY-THREE

The Shooting of James Ashley, 1998

On 15 January 1998, firearm officers in East Sussex shot dead a 39-year-old Liverpool man by the name of James Ashley at an address in St Leonards-on-Sea. Armed officers had attended his home address, in the belief that he was in possession of a firearm and a 'significant' quantity of drugs. He was also wanted for questioning, along with another man in relation to a stabbing.

Ashley and several of his friends rented three flats in a converted house in Western Road, St Leonards. He was suspected of being involved in the distribution of heroin, and the police had heard rumours that he also owned a gun. How strong these rumours were, or where they originated from, are unclear.

In October 1997, the premises was put under surveillance in the belief that some of the flats in the building were involved in drug dealing, but this did not lead to any subsequent raid taking place.

On 7 January 1998, Ashley was present when another man, Thomas 'Tosh' McCrudden, with whom he had been drinking, stabbed and seriously wounded another man in an argument outside a pub in Hastings town centre. All Ashley did in this instance was to pull McCrudden away from the victim after the stabbing had taken place. Over the course of the following days, armed officers were deployed throughout the area looking to locate and arrest McCrudden. Officers believed he was staying in one of the flats in Western Road. Detectives obtained a search warrant based on a tip-off from an officer in the area's Regional Crime Squad that a large quantity of cocaine had been delivered to one of the flats in the house. The officers conducting the raid were briefed that McCrudden was dangerous and known to be in the flats, and that Ashley was rumoured to be in possession of a firearm, which meant the police were authorised to use firearms. They were also told, incorrectly as it turned out, that Ashley was wanted for shooting a man in Eastbourne and had a previous conviction for attempted murder.

At 4:30am on 15 January, officers from Sussex Police executed a warrant on the Western Road address. The warrant allowed the police to search for the following: to locate and apprehend McCrudden; the retrieval of the suspected cocaine; and the seizure of the firearm that Ashley allegedly had in his possession. The search used a technique which was originally designed for hostage-rescue operations, but which had become standard practice in the Sussex Police area for rapid-style entries to locate and secure evidence. It was a potentially high-risk strategy as it involved individual officers entering a particular room before calling in backup if a threat was found. The officer who shot Ashley, PC Christopher Sherwood, had never actually undergone any training in this particular tactic. The police did not have a plan of the building and did not know which flats the individuals they were looking for actually lived in.

Ashley had been in bed when his girlfriend woke him to investigate a noise, which in reality was caused by the police as they made their way into the building to begin their search. As Ashley approached the bedroom door, he suddenly encountered one of the officers. He raised his arm, to which the officer reacted by firing a single shot at a range of about 2 feet. Ashley was hit in the armpit and the bullet travelled to his heart, killing him almost immediately. McCrudden was not found to be in any of the flats that were searched during the raid, neither were any firearms or drugs.

The incident led to not one, but two inquiries being carried out by other police forces under the auspices of the Police Complaints Authority (PCA). Neither inquiry produced a report that was complimentary for Sussex Police, with one being extremely critical of some of the force's most senior officers, with the other talking about the inadequate training of some of the officers who had carried out the raid.

In 2001, at the Central Criminal Court of the Old Bailey, the officer who fired the fatal shot, PC Christopher Sherwood, was charged with murder but was later acquitted on the grounds of self-defence. Mrs Justice Anne Rafferty directed the jury to find him not guilty. Sherwood had claimed self-defence, giving evidence to the court that he had feared for his life, believing that based on the briefing for the operation, Ashley's outstretched arm was holding a firearm and that he was about to shoot. In directing the jury, the judge stated that no evidence had been presented that Sherwood had fired in anything other than self-defence, and in her summing up suggested that 'those who should be held accountable were not present' in her court. Other officers were charged with misconduct in public office in relation to the incident, at Wolverhampton Crown Court, but they were also acquitted when the Crown Prosecution Service offered no evidence against any of the officers. Nigel Sweeney, for the prosecution, informed the court that the depth of 'corporate failing' within Sussex Police made it impossible to place criminal liability with individual officers. Following the verdict, Ashley's family announced their intention to sue Sussex Police for negligence.

This was a case that certainly did not reflect well on Sussex Police, and instead greatly damaged their reputation for several years.

In 2001, reporter Nick Davies wrote an article for *The Guardian* showing that during the previous ten years, police throughout England and Wales had shot a total of forty-one individuals who turned out not to be in possession of a firearm. It also showed that fifteen of these were fatal shootings and that in twenty-eight of the forty-one incidents, the individual who was shot possessed an imitation firearm, or some other kind of weapon. Six of these shootings came about following an officer's accidental discharging their firearm, which left six other incidents, including the one in which James Ashley was shot. Damming as these facts are, they also highlight the inherent dangers faced by police officers when they carry firearms during police operations.

In 2003, the same year Ashley's family was given a public apology by the police for his death, the PCA recommended stronger control of armed operations and equipping armed officers with less lethal options of dealing with suspects, such as TASER.

CHAPTER TWENTY-FOUR

The Shooting of Azelle Rodney, 2005

The shooting of Azelle Rodney by police on 30 April 2005 is quite possibly one of the most controversial police shootings of all time. Not because Rodney was shot and killed, but because the police officer who shot him was subsequently charged with his murder more than nine years after the shooting had taken place.

On the evening of 30 April, Rodney, along with two other men, were in a Volkswagen Golf that was being driven through north London. What none of the men in the vehicle knew was that they were being followed by three unmarked police vehicles containing members of the Metropolitan Police's elite Specialist Firearms Command, also known as CO19. What Rodney and the other two men also did not know was that they had been under police surveillance for two days, and that leading up to them being stopped, their every move had been followed by the police for several hours.

The briefing the firearms officers received before being deployed on the operation included the fact that the suspects were believed to be in possession of three model 10 submachine guns, better known as Mac-10s, an extremely deadly weapon that could fire up to 1,500 rounds per minute.

The decision to stop the suspects' vehicle was taken and it was boxed in by the three unmarked police vehicles following it at approximately 7:45pm in Hale Lane, Barnet. During the stop, one of the police firearms officers leant across from the front passenger seat of the vehicle and aimed his Heckler & Koch G36 semi-automatic carbine at Rodney, who was sat in the rear of his vehicle. Rather than raise his hands, it is alleged that Rodney leant down into the footwell of the car, and so the police firearms officer fired eight times, with six of the rounds striking Rodney in the face, head, neck and chest. The other two men in the car were both uninjured and were arrested by other members of the team.

An immediate search of the suspects' vehicle discovered live ammunition, a .45 calibre Colt M1911 semi-automatic handgun, and a Russian Baikal pistol, along with a much smaller gun described as being no bigger than a key fob, all of which were found in the rear of the vehicle where Rodney had been sitting.

An officer only has to believe that his life or that of another is in imminent danger before he can justifiably discharge his firearm. The person the officer is shooting at does not have to be armed for that belief to be complete.

Rodney's two accomplices, 26-year-old Wesley Lovell and 24-year-old Frank Graham, were subsequently found guilty of firearms charges and sentenced to seven years and six years respectively. Lovell's flat was also being used to make crack cocaine, and in some quarters, the sentences the men received were seen as being extremely lenient.

As was routine procedure for such incidents, the matter was investigated by the Independent Police Complaints Commission (IPCC), who in turn passed their findings on to the Crown Prosecution Service (CPS). In July 2006, the CPS announced that no police officer would face any charges in relation to the death of Azelle Rodney, but this was not to be the end of the case.

At a pre-inquest hearing heard at Hornsey Coroners' Court on 2 August 2007, before Her Majesty's deputy coroner for the north district of Greater London, it was confirmed that there was an obligation to conduct an inquest into the killing of Azelle Rodney under Section (3) (b) of the Coroners' Act 1988, whilst under Article 2 of the European Convention on Human Rights, there was a duty on the state to investigate a death caused by an agent of the state.

Rodney's inquest was due to take place later the same day, also at the Coroners' Court in Hornsey, but it was adjourned after the deputy coroner, Andrew Walker, ruled that a full inquest into Rodney's death could not go on because the available police officer's statements were so heavily redacted. There was no suggestion of any impropriety on behalf of the police, however, because the redactions were made in keeping with the terms and conditions of the Regulation of Investigatory Powers Act 2000, which covers information that has been obtained from covert surveillance, telephone taps and tracking devices.

In May 2009, Rodney's mother, Susan Alexander, took the British government to the European Court of Human Rights, claiming that her human rights had been breached by their failure to hold a 'reasonably prompt' and public investigation into her son's death. This resulted in an apology by the government to the European Court of Human Rights for the delay in investigating the full circumstances into her son's death.

Lord Bach, the then Justice Minister, made an announcement on 30 March 2010 in the House of Lords that there was to be a public inquiry into the shooting of Azelle Rodney. This was the first time in English legal history that a public inquiry had replaced an inquest jury in investigating and deciding upon the outcome in relation to a killing of a citizen by an agent of the state.

The public inquiry officially opened on 6 October 2010 and was held under the chairmanship of Sir Christopher Holland, but it would be nearly two years, on 3 September 2012, before the first oral evidence in the case was heard. The officer who fired the shots that killed Rodney, and was now retired, was one of those who gave evidence, and with his identity protected he was referred to by his call sign on the day of the shooting (Echo) E7. The officer told the inquiry he had shot Rodney because his movements led him to believe that he had picked up a weapon, possibly a machine gun, and that he was about to open fire. He added that at no point had he ever claimed to have seen Rodney holding a gun, because his view of Rodney's hands had been obscured by the car door.

The public inquiry into the killing of Rodney, which concluded in July 2013, makes for an extremely interesting read, with the Executive Summary of the inquiry's report making several assumptions concerning the actions of officer E7.

Although the full report is available online, what follows are just a few of the salient points - some of which are hard to fathom.

Point 26. Mentions that officer E7 fired his first shot 0.06 seconds after the vehicle he was travelling in stopped immediately alongside the vehicle Rodney was in, but it does not appear to make any allowance for the time between when E7 first had sight of Rodney and his movements, and when he opened fired, a time difference that has to be relevant. It also points out that the first six shots fired by E7 took only 1.11 seconds. Why that is mentioned, or what inference it is trying to suggest, is not explained. What it does show is what an excellent firearms officer E7 was.

Point 30. Begins with the almost inflammatory statement that, 'E7's accounts of what he saw are not to be accepted. Prior to firing he did not believe that the man who turned out to be Azelle Rodney had picked up a gun and was about to use it.' That is exactly what E7 believed and is the very reason he opened fire.

Point 31. Includes the amazing statement that, 'even had E7 believed, for good reason, that Azelle Rodney presented a threat to his life or that of his colleagues such that it was proportionate to open fire on him with a lethal weapon. The answer is that he did not.' How the inquiry's chairman came to that conclusion and what he based that statement on, is unclear.

Point 32. Includes the following: 'Even if it was proportionate to open fire at all, there would have been no basis for firing the fatal fifth to eighth shots.' This shows a total lack of understanding of how police firearms operate. Nowhere in any police policy document or guidance, either at force or national level, does it state that an officer can only fire a certain number of shots at a suspect before they must stop. The reality is that an officer will continue to fire at a suspect as long as they believe they still pose a threat to their life, their colleagues' lives or those of members of the public. That is exactly what E7 did in this case, which leads to the question as to who was it that decided that 'even if it was proportionate to open fire at all, there would have been no basis for firing the fatal fifth to eighth shots.' It is an extremely misleading and damaging observation to make.

Point 35. 'The MPS chose to provide legal representation for itself as well as for the officers involved in Operation Tayport, save for E7, although the officer did subsequently have a barrister provided for them by the Metropolitan Police Federation. It failed to distinguish between its responsibility as an employer, to support its staff, and its responsibility for operations.' Only the MPs know why they chose not to provide legal representation for E7; a decision which one can only imagine must have been totally devastating for the officer, potentially leaving him with feelings of uncertainty, or the betrayal of being hung out to dry by the very organisation he would have expected to support him.

The report also went on to say that the police officer who killed Rodney, 'could not be rationally believed' and rejected his version of events, although it went on to contradict itself by saying that he was 'not deliberately lying'. Lying is lying, an individual is either lying or telling the truth. The report also contradicted itself when it said that firing at Rodney to kill him 'was disproportionate and therefore unreasonable and unlawful', despite the fact that the officer had previously said he had believed Rodney was in the process of picking up a firearm, possibly a machine gun, which he had been informed might be in the vehicle.

There is one final anomaly with the report, when it states that the first two shots that struck Rodney had neutralised any threat from him, meaning that the subsequent shots fired by the officer 'were unlawful, either causing death or being fired at a dead or dying man'. If as the inquiry states that Rodney was neutralised by the first two shots, a polite way of saying he had been killed, how could the subsequent shots have been unlawful? The officer did not fire two or three separate bursts at Rodney, stopping between each burst, but fired eight rounds in 2.1 seconds. In essence, it could be interpreted that the officer was charged with murder because he fired four rounds into a man who was, by the inquiry's own admission, already dead, although under the Criminal Attempts Act 1981, 'a person may be guilty of attempting to commit an offence even though the facts are such that the commission of the offence is impossible.' But as far as the officer was concerned, he was lawfully taking somebody's life in an attempt to save his own, along with the lives of his colleagues, and was therefore not committing any offence, and certainly not one of murder.

E7, the officer who had shot and killed Rodney, was understandably not happy with the inquiry's findings. Supported by the Metropolitan Police Commissioner, the officer applied to the High Court for a judicial review of the public inquiry, claiming that the chairman's conclusions in the report were 'irrational'. However, Mr Justice Williams, in refusing to conduct a review of the public inquiry, said he had 'no doubt' there was 'ample evidence to justify the finding that E7 did not have an honest belief that Mr Rodney had picked up a gun'. Once again, an outrageous statement to make, especially as E7 had previously said that is exactly what he did have.

The inquiry's report referred the case to the CPS to decide whether or not the officer should be prosecuted for the murder of Azelle Rodney. On 30 July 2014, it was announced by the CPS that E7 would be charged with murder, saying 'there is a realistic prospect of conviction and that a prosecution was in the public interest.' At this time, reporting restrictions were lifted and the ex-officer was publicly named as Anthony Long.

The trial started at the Central Criminal Court of the Old Bailey on 8 June 2015, some ten years after Rodney's death. On 3 July, Anthony Long was found not guilty of murder and cleared by the jury with a majority verdict, who had not been informed of the public inquiry's conclusion that Azelle Rodney's killing was unlawful, and that PC Long had previously shot and killed two other individuals in the line of duty during his time as a police firearms officer, as well as shooting and wounding two other suspects.

The judge's key question to the members of the jury during his summing up at the end of the trial was as follows: 'Have the prosecution made us sure that, at the time that he fired his first shot, the defendant did not genuinely believe (even if mistakenly) that he and/or others were about to be fired at, so that he needed to defend himself and/or others by firing at Mr Rodney? If the answer is no, then you have reached a verdict of not guilty.'

The obvious, and somewhat alarming, question here is, why did the CPS not use the same benchmark when initially deciding to charge PC Long with murder?

After the trial, Long declared, 'Police firearms officers do not go out intending to shoot people and, like me in this case, have to make split-second life or death decisions based on the information available to them at the time.'

The Azelle Rodney case highlighted the everyday pressures and dangers that police firearms officers face. The amount of stress PC Long must have been under during this period can only be guessed

at, but the question that must be asked is whether it is right that any man should have to endure a ten-year wait to be tried for a crime of murder.

Any firearms officer in a similar situation has to make a split-second decision as to whether or not they pull the trigger of their firearm, and although it is the last thing they ever want to do, they have to be prepared to do so if the circumstances dictate it. Although that decision will differ from officer to officer, it does not mean any of them are wrong, it just means that individuals will see things differently, react differently and because of that, some of them will kill whilst others will be killed.

On a warm sunny day in July 2024, I met up with Tony Long at a London Hotel. Although we had never met, I recognised him as soon as he appeared through the hotel's revolving front doors. We were both retired police officers in their mid-sixties, who had been firearms officers for their respective forces. In our younger days, we had both had a full head of ginger hair, a colour neither of us had been for a number of years. Our sons served in His Majesty's Armed Forces, but that is where our similarities ended. In a firearms sense, we were light years apart. Tony Long was the consummate firearms officer during his years serving as a Constable in the Metropolitan Police.

I found him to be an intelligent, engaging and educated individual. A man who was calmness personified and somebody who oozed self-confidence, whilst being neither arrogant nor conceited.

The main reason I had wanted to reach out to Tony was to find out about how he had dealt with the situation mentally, in the aftermath of the Azelle Rodney shooting, with the rollercoaster of changing decisions that had been made in the ten years between the time of the shooting and his trial for murder. For somebody to have that level of stress hanging over their head for so long could not have been easy, and for many, it would have undoubtedly broken them. It must be remembered that it is not just the officer concerned who is affected. It is their family, friends and work colleagues as well. What is more, if Tony Long had been found guilty of murder, he would have been looking at a life sentence, not a pleasant experience for anybody, especially a retired police officer who had been convicted of killing a member of the public. When I asked him how he had managed to keep it all together and not crack under the pressure, his answer was somewhat surprising, whilst at the same time being straight-forward, honest and to the point.

'I knew I was innocent, and that's what I kept focusing on.'

We chatted away, our conversation interrupted only by the periodical delivery of cups of cappuccino, mochas and a light lunch. The time flew by and before we knew it, five hours had passed, and it was now time for us to part company and go our separate ways.

After our meeting, I was left with the belief that the British government urgently needs to address the issue of police-related shootings, not just the current legal situation, but how the aftermath of such incidents are dealt with. It simply cannot be right that officers are being taken to court, or face disciplinary proceedings, up until ten years after the original events took place. It would be totally unacceptable for a member of the public to be dealt with in the same way. Politicians, the press and even large sections of the general public would be shouting from the roof tops about 'abuse of due process' and how unfair the system was, and rightly so.

CHAPTER TWENTY-FIVE

The Shooting of Jean Charles de Menezes, 2005

Jean Charles de Menezes was born on 7 January 1978, in Gonzaga, Brazil, and arrived in England on 13 March 2002 on a six month's visitor's visa. When this expired, he applied to remain in the country as a student and was granted permission to remain in the country until 30 June 2003, but after this, rather than return to Brazil, he chose to remain in the country. He was shot dead by police on the London underground at Stockwell tube station on 22 July 2005, after he had been wrongly identified as being involved in a terrorist-related incident that had taken place the previous day, which in turn was in reaction to another terrorist incident that had taken place two weeks earlier, on 7 July, when fifty-two innocent members of the public had been killed during the London bombings.

The possibility of British police having to confront and deal with a suicide bomber had only become a topic of serious discussion after the attacks on the Twin Towers in New York on 11 September 2001. This resulted in guidelines which identified the safest and most effective way of dealing with terrorist suspects and was given the code name of Operation Kratos. It was based in the main on the experience and advice of Israeli security services. One aspect of the guidelines is the shooting of a suspect who has no apparent intent of surrendering in the head, so as to prevent them from carrying out their act of terrorism. Normal police tactics, if called upon to discharge their firearms, is to shoot at the suspect's torso. Aiming at a terrorist suspect's head is done for two reasons. Firstly, in case they are wearing a suicide vest, firing at their torso risks hitting and detonating it. Secondly, aiming at the head will likely kill them immediately, which is essential in the circumstances so that they do not detonate their vest. This is also one of the reasons why, when dealing with a terror suspect who is, or is believed to be, wearing a suicide vest, an armed officer is unlikely to shout out 'armed police', because to do so would alert the suspect and give them time to detonate their vest, thus placing the general public in danger.

There is no legal requirement for a police firearms officer to give a warning before they open fire, although guidelines published by the Association of Chief Police Officers say that it should be considered. That by its very nature is always going to differ from operation to operation. A police firearms officer is placed in a hideous position when dealing with a potential terrorist suspect, whether they are wearing a suicide vest or not. If they are and the officer takes too long to react, the terrorist could detonate their vest and kill or injure the officers confronting them, along with civilians in the immediate vicinity. If they do open fire and the suspect was wearing a suicide vest, or a fake one, nothing further would be said, but if the suspect was not wearing one and a police officer shot and killed them, they could face a charge of murder. The officer would usually only have a few seconds to make up their mind as to what they should do for the best, with their safety and that of members of the public at the forefront of their thinking.

On 21 July 2005, four attempted terrorist bombing incidents had taken place in London as a follow-up to the previous bombings that had occurred on 7 July. No suspects had been killed or captured in the immediate aftermath of the attacks, forcing the Metropolitan Police to launch a massive manhunt, whilst also dealing with the protentional threat that those responsible would look to make further attacks.

A bag containing one of the unexploded bombs had been recovered from one of the crime scenes. Somewhat unbelievably, inside the bag one of the bombers had left a gym membership card, which included the owner's home address in block of flats on Scotia Road in Tulse Hill. The police placed the flats under surveillance, one of which was occupied by Jean Charles de Menezes and two of his cousins. At about 9:30am on the morning of 22 July, Menezes left the block via the main entrance and was spotted by a surveillance officer referred to in the Stockwell 1 report as 'Frank'. This same individual was identified from the inquest into the shooting of Menezes as being a soldier, meaning that he would have been a special forces operative, or someone of a similar standing. His actual name has never been revealed.

Frank, who had in his possession photographs of the previous day's suspects, recovered from CCTV footage, quickly compared what he had in front of him with Menezes and decided that he required a closer look. As he had been urinating at the time he spotted him, Frank was unable to video Menezes, which meant that he could not send an image of him to the Metropolitan Police's operational headquarters for major incidents.

Without video footage of Menezes to look at and compare, the person in overall charge of the operation, Gold Commander Cressida Dick, had an extremely difficult decision to make, which had only been compounded by the surveillance officers being unable to video Menezes, or to positively identify him, which ultimately led to his eventual shooting at Stockwell station.

Menezes was an electrician by trade and had received a phone call telling him to go to a job. This was the reason he left his flat, although he was not carrying any tools or a bag when he did.

Cressida Dick gave the order to her surveillance officers on the ground to follow Menezes and under no circumstances were they to allow him to get onto the Underground network. Not long after he had left, Menezes caught a bus from one of the stops on Tulse Hill. With the benefit of hindsight, the decision to let him catch a bus appears to have been an extremely strange one, taking into account that one of the previous day's bombings had taken place on a bus, and there were members of the public on board who were potentially just as much at risk as those subsequently on the train at Stockwell station. If there was a concern about him getting the Underground, then surely there should have been the same level of concern about him boarding a bus for a journey of just over 2 miles.

It was during the bus journey from Tulse Hill to Stockwell station that a member of the unarmed surveillance team who had followed Menezes onto the bus, contacted the operations Gold Command to inform them that Menezes potentially matched two of the suspects they were looking for. This was possibly another mistake, in so far as the surveillance team should have been armed because if Menezes *was* a suicide bomber, the officers would not have been in a position to prevent him from detonating his bomb.

On receiving the information about Menezes, Cressida Dick instructed the surveillance team to detain him as soon as possible, which was to be before he entered the Underground. Possibly because they were not armed, this did not happen, and after alighting from the bus, Menezes made his way into Stockwell station. It was only then that Metropolitan firearms officers from the Specialist Firearms Command, or CO19, were dispatched to that location.

Menezes arrived at the station at just after 10am and made his was down to the platform before boarding the next train. Unbeknown to him, three of those who also got on the train at the station were plain-clothed surveillance officers, one of whom sat a couple of seats away from him, whilst the other two remained standing.

Before the doors closed and the train pulled away, the Metropolitan police firearms officers arrived on the platform and the door was kept open for them by one of the surveillance officers. As the firearms officers entered the train, it is alleged that one of the surveillance officers called out 'he's there' and pointed at Menezes. Because Operation Kratos rules had already been authorised by Gold Command, Menezes was always going to be killed because in such circumstances, it is strongly believed that once a suspect realises that they have been identified by the authorities, they will immediately detonate their suicide vest. Consequently, once the surveillance officer had said to the firearms team, 'he's there', they had no other option than to open fire.

At this stage of proceedings, the surveillance operative who had been sat near to Menezes took hold of him, pinning his arms to his side. A shot rang out from one of the firearms officers, fired at close range, which struck Menezes in his face and head. The noise of the shot was heard most clearly by the unarmed surveillance officer, who was then dragged away from Menezes before more shots were fired at him. In total eleven shots were fired by two officers, but despite the closeness of their position to Menezes, three of their shots still missed. Seven hit him in the head and another in the shoulder.

As is usual in such circumstances, several civilian witnesses to the incident provided differing accounts as to what happened: how many shots had been fired, what the police had or had not said before opening fire, even down to the times between each group of shots.

Senior officers from the Metropolitan Police wasted no time in making a post-shooting press announcement admitting that it had been directly connected to the previous day's attempted bombings. They also revealed that the firearms officers had been ordered to aim and fire directly towards the suspect's head to prevent an accidental detonation of any suicide vest they might have been wearing. In keeping with this, it subsequently emerged that the SO19 officers who shot Menezes had used hollow-point bullets.

Such bullets are used by police forces throughout the UK an armed assailant needs to be stopped quickly, while minimising any risk of the bullet passing through the suspect and injuring an innocent member of the public. A full metal jacket bullet is more likely to do this while still retaining lethal force. The chief officer of a UK police force can have his officers use whichever ammunition they might consider to be appropriate for the particular circumstances of any given operation.

Immediately after the shooting, the Commissioner of the Metropolitan Police, Sir Ian Blair, telephoned the chairman of the IPCC, and also wrote a letter to the Home Office, explaining that he had instructed his officers that 'the shooting that has just occurred at Stockwell is not to be referred to the IPCC and that they will be given no access to the scene at the present time.' The letter Sir Ian sent to the Home Office was subsequently released by the Metropolitan Police, but only after a request had been made under the Freedom of Information Act. Sir Ian stated that it was his intention to protect the tactics used by the Metropolitan Police as well as the sources of information which had been used from the general public, because not to do so would jeopardise future such operations.

The Menezes case stayed in the news long after his shooting. Initially there were demonstrations both in Brazil and London by family members, friends, and various different groups. Then the Brazilian government demanded explanations concerning the circumstances which led to one of their citizens being shot. The police apologised to the Menezes family for the death of their son, but the family rejected it and condemned the shooting.

Amongst the madness that followed in the days after Menezes shooting, a moment of sanity managed to surface when, on 23 August, Dania Gorodi, the sister of Michelle Otto, a Romanian who was killed in the London bombings of 7 July 2005, asked for the criticism of the Commissioner of the Metropolitan Police, Sir Ian Blair, over the Menezes shooting to stop because she felt the media focus had been taken away from the bombings of 7 and 21 July. 'People have lost sight of the bigger picture,' she said. 'We need to support the police right now, not crucify one man. This is unprecedented in British history. Sir Ian is doing the best he can.'

On 4 August 2005, *The Guardian* included an article which claimed the newly formed military unit, the Special Reconnaissance Regiment (SRR), a special forces unit that specialised in covert surveillance, had also been involved in the operation that led to the shooting of Menezes. The anonymous source for the article had come from a 'Whitehall official', who stressed that the SRR had only been involved in intelligence gathering, and that Menezes was shot by armed police, not by members of the SRR or other soldiers. Further newspaper articles which followed stated that it was believed members of the SRR were also present on the underground train when Menezes was shot.

On 16 August, the Menezes family campaign, Justice4Jean called for an enquiry into the shooting.

It was announced by the IPCC on 14 March 2006 that the first part of their inquiry, known as 'Stockwell 1', was complete and that the report's recommendations had been passed on to the Metropolitan Police Authority and Crown Prosecution Service. However, the IPCC also announced that the report 'could not be made public until all legal processes have concluded'. The report referred to was eventually published on 8 November 2007.

In July 2006, the Crown Prosecution Service (CPS) stated that there was insufficient evidence to prosecute any named individual police officers in a personal capacity, but that a criminal prosecution of the Commissioner of the Metropolitan Police would be brought under the Health & Safety at Work Act 1974, on the failure of a duty of care that was due to Menezes. On 14 December 2006, an application by the Menezes family for a judicial review to be carried out into the decision of the office of the Director of Public Prosecutions (DPP) on behalf of the CPS not to bring criminal prosecutions against any of the individual police officers who shot Menezes was unanimously rejected, ruling that 'It was a reasonable decision ... on the basis that they were likely to fail'.

On 1 November 2007, the Metropolitan Police Commissioner was found guilty under the Health & Safety at Work Act 1974, and his office was fined £175,000, together with £385,000 of legal costs.

The inquest into the Menezes shooting began at the Oval cricket ground in London on 22 September 2008, and concluded on 12 December, with the jury returning an open verdict.

On 10 June 2015, the Menezes family took the British government to the European Court of Human Rights following its decision to not prosecute anybody for the killing of Jean Charles. This was brought under Article 2 of the Human Convention on Human Rights. On 30 March 2016, the court's Grand Chamber found that the British government had not breached Article 2.

The reality of the incident always dictated that neither of the firearms officers who shot Menezes was ever going to be prosecuted for his death. If they had been, the repercussions for the Metropolitan Police and the British government would have been far reaching and could have resulted in the long-term ineffectiveness of police forces to react to similar circumstances in the future. Tragic as it was, the death of Menezes was not the fault of the firearms officers. They were acting on the information and instructions given to them by senior police officers within the Metropolitan Police, based on the belief, albeit an incorrect one, that they were dealing with a terrorist who was possibly wearing a suicide vest and had boarded the train to detonate it.

CHAPTER TWENTY-SIX

The Shooting of Raoul Moat, 2010

Raoul Thomas Moat had worked as a bouncer at different venues in and around the Newcastle area, a job which suited the heavily built 37-year-old. He was a man who was reasonably well known to the police, having been arrested a dozen times between 2000 and 2010. His first arrest was for conspiracy to commit murder, but despite the seriousness of the offence, and after being interviewed about the matter, he was released without charge.

In 2005 he was back in court charged with possessing a Japanese Samurai sword and a knuckle duster. Once again, despite the seriousness of the offence, he was acquitted.

In February 2010 Moat once again found himself as a defendant in a court room, this time charged with assaulting a 9-year-old child. On this occasion there was no acquittal, and he was found guilty and given an eighteen-week sentence at Durham prison, from where he was released on 1 July 2010. Even though he had been arrested several times, only one of his previous convictions had been connected to an act of violence, so what was about to follow was in some respects difficult to comprehend.

Moat was a father of three children, one of whom was a daughter he had with 22-year-old Samantha Stobbart, with whom he had been in a fluid relationship for more than six years. Whilst Moat was in prison, the pair had communicated with each other and just two days before he was released, Stobbart told him that their relationship was over and that she had a new partner, adding that he was a police officer, which was untrue. It is possible that she had told him this out of fear and in the hope that he would leave her and her new partner alone. It would be fair to say that Moat was no great lover of the police, so hearing that his ex-girlfriend, and the mother of his daughter, was now dating a policeman would not have been something he would have wanted to hear.

The news resulted in his behaviour becoming somewhat erratic, to such an extent that it had not only come to the attention of the prison authorities, but they had in turn taken the decision to inform Northumbria Police of their concerns about the potential threat he posed on his release.

This was difficult for the police because on the one hand they had some important intelligence about Moat, but until he actually did something, or they received more information that increased his potential threat level, there was not much they could have done.

This was also the early days of social media, which Moat wasted no time in utilising once he had left prison, posting: 'Just got out of jail, I've lost everything, my business, my property and to top it all off my lass of six years has gone off with someone else. I'm not 21 and I can't rebuild my life. Watch and see what happens.'

On Moat's release from prison, Samantha Stobbart and her new boyfriend, 29-year-old karate instructor Chris Brown, were staying at an address in Birtley, Gateshead. How Moat knew they were there is unclear, but soon after midnight on 3 July, it became apparent to those inside the property that somebody was outside. Brown went to investigate and was confronted by Moat, who produced a sawn-off shotgun, opened fire and shot Brown from close range, killing him outright. Rather than running off in a blind panic, Moat calmly approached the house, looked in through the living room window, saw Samantha Stobbart and opened fire again, hitting her in the lower stomach and one of her arms, while her mother was phoning the police. Moat did not attempt to fire anymore shots and simply slipped away into the night. Stobbart was taken to hospital to undergo major surgery, where she was placed under round-the-clock armed guard, just in case Moat, realising he had not killed her, tried to finish her off.

This led to one of the biggest manhunts in Northumbrian and British policing history. It was a massive operation, lasting for seven days. Police helicopters were used, and the RAF even became involved when they deployed a jet for reconnaissance purposes. There were 160 firearms officers from Northumbria and the surrounding policing areas involved, who had to be prepared for every eventuality simply because they had no idea where Moat was hiding. They did not know whether he was holed up in a friend's home or hiding in a wooded area. The other difficulty of course was that normal day-to-day policing also had to continue, which meant that despite the armed officers who had their specific duties in relation to the manhunt for Moat, there was a large number of officers who were going about their duties with nothing more dangerous to protect themselves with than a baton and an incapacitant spray. As usual, it was a difficult balancing act for the police, because whilst on the one hand they were looking for Moat, their most important priority was to keep the public safe, but to do this a number of their own officers were always going to be at potential risk.

Whilst he had been on the run, Moat had contacted the police stating that he would kill any officer who attempted to try to stop him. If a firearms officer had been informed of this information, it would certainly have affected how they might have subsequently dealt with him. Tensions would have been heightened, and adrenalin would have been coursing around their bodies. The margin of allowance for any movement by Moat if they had come across him would have been minimal.

Two days after the shooting, Moat resurfaced in East Denton when he approached a police vehicle at 12:45am on Sunday, 4 July. Single crewed, unarmed and defenceless, traffic officer Police Constable David Rathband was on duty in his marked vehicle, parked up on a roundabout at the junction of A1 and the A69.

Moat fired into the vehicle, hitting the officer in the face. Although he would not have known it at the time, Moat knew PC Rathband, having met him before when the officer had stopped him whilst driving a van. The chance meeting had resulted in the vehicle being confiscated as it was believed Moat had been driving it without any insurance.

Before he shot PC Rathband, Moat telephoned the police to tell them what he was about to do and phoned them back to gloat once he had carried out the shooting.

Moat's shooting of PC Rathband was nothing more than opportunist. He said killing a police officer was something that he would do, and he did it. PC Rathband survived and remained in hospital for nearly three weeks after the shooting, but was left permanently blinded in both eyes, something which he struggled to cope with as he tried to move on from the events which had cost him his sight. Twenty months later, on 29 February 2012, he took his own life.

If the police held any misconceptions about the veracity of Moat's words, they now knew that they were much more than empty threats. It must have been clear to those concerned that Moat was in control of how everything was going to end. There had been several appeals made by both the police and some of Moat's relatives for him to stop and hand himself, but sadly they all fell on deaf ears.

It cannot be emphasised just how big the operation to locate and arrest Moat became. Northumbria Police had deployed 100 of their firearms officers, while a further forty had been sent up from the

Metropolitan Police in London, and twenty from a number of other nearby forces. In an effort to allow these officers to be able to safely look for Moat, several armoured Land Rover vehicles were also sent over from the Police Service of Northern Ireland.

On 9 July, after six days on the run, Moat was finally discovered in the Craigside estate in the village of Cartington, located in central Northumberland. The area was quickly surrounded by armed police, who set up a cordon around the north bank of the River Coquet to ensure that Moat would not be able to escape, and in the hope that they would finally be able to make him surrender.

This would have been an extremely stressful time for the officers concerned. They would have no doubt been involved in the hunt for Moat on a shift-to-shift basis from the outset. They knew they were dealing with a seriously dangerous individual who had already murdered two people, including a fellow colleague, and had shot and wounded another, and who would have no doubt tried to kill again if the opportunity had arisen. Despite all this, the firearms officers were consummate professionals. There was no wild west shootout style approach as there had been with the Stephen Waldorf case in London back in January 1983. Instead, they bided their time and even engaged in six hours of negotiations with Moat in an attempt to bring the matter to a positive conclusion for all concerned, even providing him with food and drink during the stand-off in the hope that it would help to make him see sense and surrender.

At 1:15am on 10 July, two police firearms officers, who it was later revealed at the subsequent inquest into Moat's death were from West Yorkshire Police, shot Moat with a 'wireless long-range electric shock weapon', which was apparently only at an experimental stage of development and had not officially been approved for use in the UK. The projectiles contained a small high-voltage battery, which was discharged from a 12-gauge shotgun. Soon after this incident, Moat committed suicide by shooting himself in the head.

Despite what had happened previously, and regardless of how dangerous an individual Moat was, not to mention the potential threat he posed, the police firearms officers tried their very best to take Moat alive. When they finally fired at him it was by means of a non-lethal option, despite the more lethal options they had at their disposal. Having said that, throughout the entire six-hour stand-off, the only person Moat ever posed a threat to was himself. As best is known he never at any time pointed his shotgun towards any of the police officers who had surrounded him, because if he had, he would most surely have been shot. So, the police really had no other option than to deploy the tactics they did. Shooting him by means of using lethal force was never an option: as long as he posed no direct threat to anyone other than himself, there would never be any justification for shooting him.

In the days immediately after the man hunt was over, a total of twenty other individuals were arrested in connection to the shootings by Raoul Moat. Out of these, two men appeared at Newcastle Magistrates' Court on 8 July, charged with conspiracy to commit murder and possession of a firearm with intent. This came from the prosecution's belief that both men were jointly responsible for supplying Moat with the sawn-off shotgun that he subsequently used in the shootings and were in company with him when he shot PC David Rathband. It was also believed that one of them accompanied Moat when he shot his ex-girlfriend Samantha Stobbart and her partner Chris Brown. When the case ended, one of the men, having been found guilty as charged, received three life sentences with a recommendation that he serve a minimum of forty years' imprisonment, whilst the other man, who was also found guilty, received a sentence of two life sentences with a recommendation that he serve a minimum of twenty years' imprisonment.

CHAPTER TWENTY-SEVEN

The Shooting of Anthony Grainger, 2012

An aspect of police-related shootings that often seems to be overlooked by the general public is the length of time, sometimes even years, it can take for an incident to be completely resolved, which is certainly unfair on the officers involved. The shooting of Anthony Grainger by an officer of the Greater Manchester Police on 3 March 2012, is one such case.

Grainger had first come to the attention of the police in September 2011 when he was suspected of being involved in the theft of a memory stick from the home of an unnamed detective of the Greater Manchester Police. The officer concerned had left the back door to his house unlocked, and an unknown intruder had simply walked in and stolen his wallet and car keys, before then driving off in the officer's car. The memory stick, which had been inside the officer's wallet, was not password protected or encrypted, which, considering it apparently contained the names of more than 1,000 police informants, was quite remarkable. If it fell into the wrong hands, it could literally have put the lives of those informants at risk.

Sometime after this event, Grainger placed items for sale on eBay, which were believed to have come from the detective's stolen vehicle. He was arrested and interviewed about the items he had put up for sale. If they did turn out to be from the detective's stolen car, the police could also then link Grainger to the theft of the memory stick. However, he made no admissions about having had any involvement in the burglary at the detective's home. In January 2012, Greater Manchester Police completed their enquiries into the case, which resulted in Grainger being cleared as they could find no solid evidence against him. But this was not the end of the matter as far as the police was concerned. Within a matter of days of clearing Grainger from their inquiries, Greater Manchester Police placed him and some of his known associates under covert surveillance as it was believed they were involved in organised crime. Such was the intelligence on the group that the officers who were tasked with carrying out the surveillance were authorised to carry firearms for their own protection.

On 3 March 2012, Anthony Grainger was sat in a stolen Audi motor vehicle, along with two other males, in Culcheth, Cheshire. Greater Manchester Police claimed they were in possession of intelligence that intimated Grainger, and his two associates were 'imminently' going to carry out a robbery, and that they should be arrested to prevent this from taking place. As officers moved in to carry out the arrests, one of them fired a single shot from a Heckler & Koch MP5 semi-automatic carbine. The bullet passed through the vehicle's windscreen, striking and killing Grainger as it passed through his heart and lungs. He was unarmed at the time of the shooting and was sat in the driver's seat of the vehicle. The other two occupants were unharmed, and no weapons were found.

The inquest into the shooting of Anthony Grainger was opened by Nicholas Rheinberg at Warrington Coroners' Court on 5 March 2012 but then adjourned to allow the Independent Police Complaints Commission (IPCC) to carry out and complete their investigation into the shooting. The investigation was concluded in July the following year, but the IPCC was far from complimentary of the police's actions. The report included the fact that the intelligence gathered as part of Operation Shire, the surveillance of Grainger and his associates, was 'flawed'. It also criticised the control of the firearms team who were sent forward to carry out of the arrests and went even further by stating that the officer who actually fired the fatal shot that killed Grainger could quite possibly end up facing a charge of manslaughter.

The IPCC report was subsequently forwarded to the Crown Prosecution Service (CPS), which decided that the police officer who fired the fatal shot would not be prosecuted, as they deemed that the jury would likely determine he had acted in self-defence and used what he believed to be appropriate force.

In his position as Chief Constable of Greater Manchester Police, Peter Fahy was charged under the Health and Safety at Work Act 1974 in relation to the level of preparation leading up to the operation. If found guilty, the likely penalty faced by Greater Manchester Police was an unlimited fine.

In January 2015 Greater Manchester Police made an application at Liverpool Crown Court to have the case against them dropped, arguing an abuse of process. The argument was based on the fact that the evidence that needed to be disclosed in open court for Fahy to be given a fair trial would not be in the public interest and would also prejudice further operations by the force. The argument was accepted by the judge, which left the CPS with no option but to accept this decision and drop the case.

Four years after the fatal shooting of Anthony Grainger, in March 2016, the then Home Secretary, Theresa May, announced the inquest into his death would now become a statutory public inquiry, which meant that all relevant evidence would be heard, including confidential police documents which had previously been deemed as too sensitive to be disclosed.

A preliminary hearing to outline the parameters of the inquiry began in November 2016, and the public inquiry into the shooting of Anthony Grainger was opened the following January, under the auspices of Judge Teague, who had been the coroner in charge of the original inquest.

In July 2019, more than seven years after the original shooting, the public inquiry finally issued its report, which was far from complimentary of the Greater Manchester Police. Part of the report criticised them for the shooting, stating that there were serious deficiencies in its firearms unit.

The length of time this case took to be finalised was unfair, unacceptable and no doubt extremely stressful both for Anthony Grainger's family, the officer who fired the shots, and his immediate family. It could also be argued that the general public had a right to know the full facts about what had transpired leading up to the shooting of Grainger.

Such cases only appear to take so long to be finalised when it involves the shooting of a member of the public by a police officer. In a similar matter involving two members of the public, or if a member of the public shot and killed a serving police officer, it would never be allowed to take so long to be fully resolved. Some of the delays could be regarded as understandable, but even so, seven years is still an awfully long time. It is amazing how an officer in such circumstances not only manages to cope with the wait to find out what is going to happen to them, but also how they are able to affectively function as a serving police officer. After all, it is almost certain that the officer concerned would not have been allowed to return to firearms duties, although whether they might have wanted to under such circumstances is a different matter.

CHAPTER TWENTY-EIGHT

The Shooting of Jermaine Baker, 2015

On 11 December 2015, 28-year-old Jermaine Baker, along with two other men, was sat in a stolen Audi car in Wood Green, London, not far from the local Crown Court building. It was believed that the men were waiting to help free two other men who were being transported from Wormwood Scrubs to Wood Green Crown Court for a sentencing hearing in connection to firearms offences.

The Metropolitan Police had discovered the men's plan and were lying in wait in unmarked vehicles. They were also in possession of information that the men apparently had access to firearms. To this end, the surveillance officers from the Met's Organised Crime Command, who had been deployed on the operation, had been authorised to carry firearms. Police surrounded the vehicle that Baker and his associates were in at 9am, and soon after a single shot, fired by one of the officers, only identified by his call-sign W80, rang out. The bullet struck Baker, who was sat in the front passenger seat of the vehicle, in the wrist and neck, and he died approximately an hour and a half later. Baker was unarmed at the time of the shooting, although a replica Uzi submachine gun was subsequently discovered in the car.

The shooting was investigated by representatives of the Independent Police Complaints Commission (IPCC) and the inquiry quickly picked up a head of steam. On 14 December, just three days after the shooting, the police officer who shot Baker was suspended by the Metropolitan Police at the request of the IPCC because they had determined that the matter was being dealt with as a 'homicide'. How the IPCC had come to this decision remained unexplained, and even the Metropolitan Police was given no explanation as to how that decision had been achieved, but despite this lack of transparency on the part of the IPCC, the Metropolitan Police still went ahead and acquiesced to the request to suspend the officer.

At what would have been an extremely difficult, stressful and emotional time for the officer and his family, he would have no doubt expected some kind of support or backing from his senior officers. Instead, he was suspended. At such a time, having the support from one's colleagues is very important for the officer concerned. As if being suspended was not bad enough, three days after his suspension, the officer was arrested and interviewed under caution by members of the IPCC. However, it could also be argued that by acting so swiftly, there could be no accusations by the public, concerned groups, or Baker's family that his shooting was not been taken seriously by the authorities.

An interesting aspect of the IPCC's investigation was the discovery that the Metropolitan Police had placed a covert listening device, consisting of a miniature radio transmitter and a microphone, in Baker's vehicle. The device recorded the occupants saying that they were not in possession of a real weapon. For some inexplicable reason, this information was not passed on to the armed officers who had been deployed to make the arrest. Instead, the officers were informed that the occupants of the vehicle were armed. There is a subtle difference between those two statements.

It is unclear as to whether the Metropolitan Police informed the IPCC about the listening device in the suspect's vehicle, or whether the IPCC actually discovered the device during their examination of the car.

After completing their investigation, in November 2016 the IPCC, believing that a criminal offence may have taken place, sent their report to the Crown Prosecution Service (CPS). Seven months later, in June 2017, and after having fully digested the IPCC's report, the CPS decided that officer W80, the man who had shot Baker, would not be charged with a criminal offence, which logic dictates would most likely have been murder. The CPS reached this decision on the basis that there was no realistic prospect of securing a conviction as officer W80 had stated he had acted in self-defence, believing that Baker was reaching for a firearm at the time, and that the jury would have no reason to disbelieve the officer's genuinely held belief.

The decision by the CPS not to bring charges against officer W80, or anybody else involved in the case, was not well received by everybody, including the member of parliament for Tottenham, David Lammy, the constituency where Baker lived, who wrote to the Attorney General to request a review of the CPS' decision not to prosecute. Victims and their relatives also have the right to request the CPS to reconsider a decision under the Victim's Right to Review Scheme.

In March 2018, nine months after making its original decision not to prosecute officer W80, and twenty-seven months after the original shooting, the CPS confirmed its decision not to charge the officer.

After replacing the IPCC, in 2019 the Independent Office for Police Conduct (IOPC) directed the Metropolitan Police Service to bring disciplinary proceedings against officer W80 on the grounds that in shooting Baker, he had used excessive force. The Metropolitan Police and W80 successfully challenged this decision in the High Court, arguing that the IOPC had applied the wrong legal test in assessing the officer's claim of self-defence. They said that as W80 had an honest-held belief that his life was in imminent danger from

Baker, he was justified in his use of force. This finding resulted in the High Court quashing the IPOC's directive to the Metropolitan Police to bring disciplinary proceedings against W80.

The officer must have felt he was in some giant game of tennis, because no sooner had the High Court made their decision in his favour, rather than the IOPC accepting it, they took the case to the Court of Appeal, reiterating their claim that 'police officers should be sanctioned for use of force in cases where their belief that force is required, is unreasonable or irrational.' In October 2020, after listening to the arguments on both sides in the case, the Court of Appeal reversed the previous judgement made by the High Court, which allowed the IOPC's direction to the Metropolitan Police to begin disciplinary proceedings against officer W80, to stand. This decision had far-reaching ramifications for all firearms officers, because it in effect said that despite claiming they acted in self-defence, if that belief was challenged by the IOPC and determined by them to be unreasonable, they could find themselves facing disciplinary charges, despite having not been prosecuted criminally for their actions. It was almost a reverse case of double jeopardy.

The Metropolitan Police and officer W80 applied for leave to appeal the Court of Appeal's decision to allow the IOPC to direct the Metropolitan Police to begin disciplinary proceedings against the officer. The Supreme Court dismissed this appeal in July 2023, more than eight years after the shooting of Baker. Two months later, the IOPC confirmed it would once again be directing the Metropolitan Police to instigate disciplinary proceedings against W80.

This an extremely worrying decision for all police firearms officers because as it stands, if a police officer shoots a suspect in the honest belief that they believed their life or that of another was in imminent danger, but that belief subsequently turned out to be incorrect and their use of lethal force in the circumstances was then deemed to be unreasonable, they could end up facing misconduct charges. If determined to be a case of gross misconduct, this could then lead to them being sacked, despite never having been criminally prosecuted for the same action.

Despite this decision not to bring criminal charges against him, more than three years later, in June 2021, and more than six years after the shooting, a public inquiry into Jermaine Baker's death began. On the opening day of the hearing, it was suggested that Baker might have been asleep shortly before he was shot. This came about following an audio recording retrieved from the covert listening device that the police had placed on the vehicle, which picked up what was described at the subsequent public inquiry as being either loud breathing or snoring. So, three men are sat in a stolen car, and are collectively in possession of an imitation Uzi submachine gun, whilst apparently waiting to free two men who are on their way to court, and one of them is supposedly asleep. The level of adrenalin that must have been flowing through their bodies in such circumstances, and their level of heightened alertness, would suggest that it was most likely heavy breathing, as the three men mentally prepared and psyched themselves up to do what they were about to do.

The inquiry also revealed that the officer who shot Baker went missing shortly after the shooting, and that his colleagues were so concerned for his wellbeing that he was officially designated as being 'a high-risk missing person', with the belief that he had tried to commit suicide. This emphasizes the genuine stresses police officers potentially face every time they take part in a firearms operation.

The public inquiry finished with the delivery of its final report in July 2022, and although it found that the police operation involved several failings, it also found that Baker's shooting was a lawful one, showing that this was once again an example of just how unprotected police firearms officers are under the law when carrying out the extremely difficult job they volunteer to undertake.

Officer W80 was subsequently appointed as a firearms instructor with the Metropolitan Police's SCO19 firearms unit. Despite the public inquiry deciding that the shooting was lawful, the Independent Office for Police Conduct (IOPC) determined that W80 should face disciplinary proceedings, a decision the officer challenged. In July 2023, however, the UK's Supreme Court upheld the decision to go ahead with a misconduct case. If found guilty, officer W80 could be sacked from the police. At the time this book went to print, potential disciplinary proceedings against the officer concerned had still not been concluded – more than ten years after the shooting had taken place.

CHAPTER TWENTY-NINE

The Murder of PC Keith Palmer, 2017

On 22 March 2017, a terrorist incident took place outside the Palace of Westminster, London, when just after 2:30pm, a 52-year-old man by the name of Khalid Masood intentionally drove a hire car at speeds of up to nearly 80 miles per hour into pedestrians on the south side of Westminster Bridge, and after that on Bridge Street. In total more than fifty people were hurt, of which four subsequently died of their injuries. It is believed Masood had travelled to London from Birmingham three days before his attack to carry out a reconnaissance of Westminster Bridge and its surrounding area.

One of the victims was a Romanian tourist called Andreea Cristea, 31, who was hit so hard by the impact of Masood's car that she was thrown over the parapet of the bridge into the River Thames. She was knocked unconscious and suffered further injuries as a result of the fall. Fortunately, she was rescued from the cold water, but died later in hospital. The injured on the bridge included three uniformed police officers, who had earlier attended a commendation ceremony.

Not content with the death and carnage he had already committed, Masood then drove his damaged car into the perimeter fence of the Palace of Westminster. Jumping out of the vehicle, he ran through the open Carriage Gates into the palace grounds, and was confronted by an unarmed police officer, 48-year-old Keith Palmer, a member of the Metropolitan Police's Parliamentary and Diplomatic Protection Command. PC Palmer had been a police officer for fifteen years, prior to which he had served in the British Army.

At the time of the attack, Palmer was wearing a protective vest, but Mahood fatally stabbed him before he was shot dead by another police officer, believed to have been the then Secretary of State for Defence, Michael Fallon's personal protection officer.

MP Tobias Ellwood, the Foreign Minister for the Middle East and Africa, as well as paramedics, gave PC Palmer first aid treatment, but despite their best attempts, he died at the scene. PC Palmer was posthumously awarded the George Medal in the Queen's Birthday Honours in 2017. In the 2019 New Year's Honours list, six other police officers who had been involved in the same incident were all awarded the British Empire Medal, whilst another was awarded the Queen's Police Medal for Distinguished Service. Two members of NHS England were awarded the OBE, along with another police officer who received the same award.

Masood also died at the scene, despite attempts to resuscitate him by both police officers and paramedics. He had been shot three times. The first bullet struck his upper torso and was believed to be the round that killed him.

Although treated as an act of terrorism, Masood had said in a final WhatsApp message to an unknown friend that he was waging a jihad in revenge for Western military action in Muslim countries in the Middle East. He was believed by British authorities to have been acting alone, and not for any particular terrorist organisation.

An attack such as this by a lone wolf attacker shows the difficulties faced by the police, as well as throwing open the debate about whether all police officers should routinely carry firearms. Would the unarmed police officer have been killed if he had had a weapon?

There is no definitive answer to that question but it is highly unlikely he would have been stabbed if he had been carrying a firearm.

Soon after the incident was over, additional police firearms officers were sent to the scene, including Counter Terrorist Specialist Firearms Officers, who arrived in under six minutes, which by any standard was an excellent response time.

At the time of the murder of PC Palmer and the shooting of Masood, Prime Minister Theresa May was in the House of Commons and was evacuated by her security detail and taken back to Downing Street. Parliament was suspended, with the building in essence being put into lock down mode, with nobody being allowed to enter or leave the premises.

Masood had actually been on MI5's list of known individuals, having come to their attention during a 2010 investigation into a group of Islamists who were later convicted of plotting to blow up a British Territorial Army base in Luton. Despite his known connection to the group, MI5 carried out a risk assessment on Masood and it was determined that he did not pose a threat to British national security. Subsequently, his name popped up again during an investigation by MI5 into a terrorist organisation by the name of Al-Mulhajiroun, between the years 2012 and 2016.

The inquest into Masood's death, held under the direction of the Chief Coroner of England and Wales, Mark Lucraft, took place on 12 October 2018, where the jury found that Masood had been lawfully killed. The police officer responsible for his death, identified only as SA74, shot Masood after he had ignored his shouted warnings to put down his knife and had begun running towards the officer brandishing the weapon.

CHAPTER THIRTY

The Borough Market Attack, 2017

At just before 10pm on 3 June 2017, three men in a hired van deliberately drove into pedestrians on London Bridge, mounting the pavement at high speed on three separate occasions and killing two people in the process, before subsequently crashing on Borough High Street. Several Molotov cocktails were later discovered in the back of the van.

After ramming into pedestrians on the bridge, the three men in the van, Khuram Shazad Butt, Rachid Redouane and Youssef Zaghba, jumped out and ran into the nearby Borough Market, which was full of bars, restaurants and revelers enjoying a night out with friends. Without any prior warning, the three men started randomly stabbing innocent passers-by. Five people were stabbed to death in Green Dragon Court, outside the Boro Bistro pub, before the men ran back up to the High Street where they attacked and stabbed another three people. It was here that the police first became involved in the incident, when three officers were stabbed attempting to detain the suspects. The police officers were helped in their endeavors by Spanish national Ignacio Echeverria, who worked in London for the HSBC bank. Sadly, Echeverria was later stabbed to death by one of the attackers.

Incredible acts of bravery were carried out by members of the public and unarmed police alike. One man, believed to be a fan of Millwall football club, decided to fight the three suspects with nothing more than his fists when they made their way into the restaurant that he and others were eating in. He was stabbed a total of eight times in the hands, chest and head. Thankfully, he survived his injuries.

A British Transport Police officer, armed only with his baton, also took on the attackers. He too received several stab wounds, one of which caused him to temporarily lose sight in his right eye. Two off-duty Metropolitan Police Constables, Liam Jones and Stewart Henderson, who were in the area on a night out, provided first aid to some of the seriously injured members of the public, before protecting more than 150 people inside a pub then managing to evacuate them with the help of the Metropolitan Police Marine Support Unit and RNLI boats to the opposite side of the River Thames.

The incident came to an abrupt end when the three attackers decided to charge towards the armed police officers. Eight officers, three from the City of London Police and five from the Metropolitan Police, responded by firing a total of forty-six rounds, killing them instantly. A member of the public also received a minor gunshot wound by one of the rounds fired by the police. In total, the attackers had killed eight people and wounded another forty-eight, including four un-armed police officers who had bravely tried to stop the suspects. Each of the three men was found to be wearing fake suicide vests and had taped 12-inch kitchen knives to their wrists.

The fact that there was no prior warning of this incident shows just how effective and necessary police Armed Response Vehicles (ARVs) are. It was somewhere in the region of seven minutes between the first call about the incident being received by the police, and the three attackers being shot dead. It can only be guessed at as to how many more innocent members of the public, as well as unarmed police officers, would have been killed or seriously injured if ARVs had not been in existence, remembering, of course, that all of the officers who fulfil that role are volunteers. What was not widely known at the time was that Home Secretary Amber Rudd had approved the immediate deployment of a counter terrorist unit from the SAS, and that the helicopters carrying them had actually landed on London Bridge in support of the City of London and Metropolitan Police firearms officers, just in case there might be other attackers unaccounted for in the area.

A number of those who took part in the incident were recognised for their efforts. Ignacio Echeverria was posthumously awarded the George Medal for his actions, as were PC Charlie Guenigault of the Metropolitan Police and PC Wayne Marques of the British Transport Police. Other officers received the British Empire Medal, the Queen's Gallantry Medal, and the Queen's Police Medal for Distinguished Service. Several civilians were also awarded for their bravery.

CHAPTER THIRTY-ONE

The Shooting of Chris Kaba, 2022

The shooting of 23-year-old Chris Kaba by police took place on 5 September 2022 in Streatham Hill, London, and a year later a member of the Metropolitan Police's firearms unit, the officer who had fired the fatal shot that killed Kaba, was charged with his murder. The officer's trial began in October 2024.

On the day of the shooting, Kaba was driving a car that had been linked to a firearms-related incident the previous day. Unbeknown to him, he was being followed by an unmarked police vehicle and was driving directly towards a police roadblock, forcing his car to come to a halt in Kirkstall Gardens, just after 10pm. Armed police officers from a marked police vehicle approached Kaba's car on foot, and despite instructions to get out of his vehicle, not only did Kaba refuse to do so but he drove his car into one of the police vehicles positioned in the roadblock ahead of him. Not long after this, one of the armed officers who had approached Kaba opened fire with a single round that penetrated the windscreen and struck Kaba, wounding him in the process. He was treated at the scene, taken to hospital by ambulance, but died of his wounds the following day.

Sad though Kaba's death was, as is the case when anybody loses their life in such circumstances, there is a history here that is worthy of mention that will help to provide a more complete picture of what led up to the shooting.

Before any police firearms operation, the officers to be deployed are given a briefing about the need for them to be armed, and the names of any and all persons who it is believed they will be directly looking for or who they might come into contact with. If the officers are looking for a particular individual or individuals, they will be shown photographs and provided with a history of their criminality, which will include if they are known to have used or have access to firearms. This information is extremely useful and important to the officers and helps them to focus on what they are being asked to do, both for the overall safety of all involved as well as the wellbeing of the general public at large.

In 2018, four years before he was shot by police, Kaba had been arrested and charged for possessing an imitation firearm 'with intent to cause fear or violence'. He appeared at Snaresbrook Crown Court in January 2019 and after being found guilty, was sentenced to four years' imprisonment in a young offenders' institute but was actually released in 2020.

After Kaba's death, five other men were charged with conspiring with him in connection with a shooting on 30 August 2022 at a nightclub in Hackney, where the victim was shot in both legs. This particular incident had taken place just six days before Kaba was shot by police.

After the shooting on 5 September, no firearms were found either in Kaba's car, on his person or in the immediate vicinity. This fact was highlighted in numerous newspapers, as well as on other types of media platforms. Nowhere was there any mention, however, of Kaba having used his vehicle as a means of trying to escape, and in doing so placing police officers' lives in imminent danger by being struck or crushed by his car as he rammed into the police vehicles.

In the aftermath of the shooting, allegations were made, without any substantiation whatsoever, that Kaba had been shot due to the colour of his skin. This meant that not only did the officer who shot Kaba need to face a murder trial, he also stood accused of being a racist, without any substantiated evidence.

On 20 September 2023, a year after the shooting, the Crown Prosecution Service announced that it had authorised a Metropolitan Police officer to be charged with murder in relation to the death of Chis Kaba. The following morning, the police officer, only referred to at the time by the cypher NX121, appeared before Westminster Magistrates' Court, before later appearing at the Central Criminal Court of the Old Bailey. He was granted bail, but only with the condition that he lived at a named address, surrendered his passport, and did not apply for international travel documents.

The decision to charge the officer with murder sent a shockwave of concern and annoyance amongst other firearms officers, not only in the Metropolitan Police but in other forces across the UK. The Metropolitan Police has somewhere in the region of 2,500 officers who are authorised to carry firearms for operational police purposes. By the morning of 25 September 2022, around 300 firearms officers from the Metropolitan Police had informed senior officers that they needed a 'period of time to reflect' on whether they wished to continue their roles. For several officers, however, this was a short-lived response.

On 1 March 2024, officer NX121 lost his anonymity and was named for the first time as Sergeant Martyn Blake. The disclosure of the officer's name resulted in him and his family having to move home and be provided with round-the-clock protection, after it was reported that a bounty of £10,000 had been placed on his head. How many people would have to experience such prolonged trauma and distress for simply doing their job?

On 8 March 2024, Martyn Blake appeared at the Central Criminal Court of the Old Bailey in London to enter his plea of not guilty. He was again granted bail until the commencement of his trial on 2 October. The trial lasted for three weeks and resulted in the jury finding Blake not guilty of Chris Kaba's murder, after only three hours of deliberation.

The jury had not been informed of Kaba's previous gang connections, and one would imagine this decision was taken to ensure the jury were not unduly influenced. Immediately after the trial, the Metropolitan Police Service, believing there was the possibility of a potential volatile reaction to the not-guilty verdict, successfully petitioned the judge in the case to lift the restrictions on this information being made public, so that a complete picture of events was subsequently available.

Conclusion

Most police forces throughout the UK have had firearms units, of one description or another, for around fifty years. During that time, it is true that some innocent members of the public have been shot by the police who should not have been. However, the vast majority of those who were shot were deemed to have been lawful killings by such authorities as the Independent Police Complaints Commission (IPCC), the Independent Office for Police Conduct (IOPC), public inquiries, inquests and the courts.

It cannot be forgotten that during this same period, several police officers have been shot or murdered in other ways. I do not mention this in a tit-for-tat type of way, but to simply highlight the inherent dangers and difficulties being a police officer involves, regardless of whether or not they are carrying firearms.

During this same period of time, police forces and their use of firearms has become much more professional and has improved greatly. I once had the topic of the police use of firearms described by a senior officer as being a 'necessary evil', maybe because having to authorise the use of firearms, or being in overall control of an operation, without having total control over the firearms aspect, was something a number of senior officers were not entirely comfortable with. Nevertheless, they went along with it because they did not have much choice in the matter.

Once an incident has begun to unfold, and it becomes clear that a firearms response is required from the police, then somebody has to make the call. The officers carrying the firearms do what they are trained to do once authority for their attendance at an operation has been given. There is a belief held by some, however, that certain senior officers are more concerned about potential negative connotations on their own careers should shots fired by police injure or kill members of the public during an operation.

Today all police forces have got their act together in relation to their use of firearms, whether that be with the standard of training provided, the selection process of personnel wanting to become firearms officers, or the weapons and equipment provided to carry out their extremely difficult task. The attitude now is one of professionalism, preparation, and training for all eventualities, rather than simply being reactive when a firearms-related incident is reported to the police.

Sadly, one aspect, and quite possibly the most important, which has not been addressed is the part that the British government could and should play on the matter. It is accepted that it is a difficult subject to legislate for, but officers who volunteer to carry out this role within policing should expect to be given some kind of legal protection, as well as a laid-down time frame in relation to criminal and/or disciplinary proceedings being taken against them. Having said that, if officers are provided with legal protection from prosecution, then there would be no need to have to consider the timeframe aspect.

I personally enjoyed my years working as a police firearms officer. I was fortunate enough to have been involved in some very interesting operations, and I got to work with some incredible individuals who I happily stood shoulder to shoulder with in extremely testing circumstances. It is an aspect of policing that is not for everybody and not every police officer is cut out for it. The potential danger it places you in is immense, and the burden it places on your shoulders can weigh extremely heavily. What other civilian-based job is there that involves having to make a split-second decision which can literally decide whether somebody lives or dies?

Being a police firearms officer allows you to protect members of the public from the dangerous elements of society, whilst at the same time meaning you must be prepared to put your life on the line in doing so. Do I have any regrets about having been a police firearms officer? Absolutely not. I am just glad I was deemed to have the required calibre necessary to carry out the role. Would I do it all over again? In a heartbeat.

APPENDIX A

Territorial Police Forces in the UK

Avon & Somerset Constabulary
Bedfordshire Police
Cambridgeshire Constabulary
Cheshire Constabulary
City of London Police
Cleveland Police
Cumbria Constabulary
Derbyshire Constabulary
Devon & Cornwall Police
Dorset Police
Durham Constabulary
Dyfed-Powys Police
Essex Police
Gloucestershire Constabulary
Greater Manchester Police
Gwent Police
Hampshire & Isle of Wight Constabulary
Hertfordshire Constabulary
Humberside Police
Kent Police
Kew Constabulary

Lancashire Constabulary
Leicestershire Police
Lincolnshire Police
Merseyside Police
Metropolitan Police Service
Norfolk Constabulary
North Wales Police
Northamptonshire Police
Northumbria Police
North Yorkshire Police
Nottinghamshire Police
Police Service of Northern Ireland
Police Scotland
South Wales Police
South Yorkshire Police
Staffordshire Police
Suffolk Constabulary
Surrey Police
Sussex Police
Thames Valley Police
Warwickshire Police
West Mercia Police
West Midlands Police
West Yorkshire Police
Wiltshire Police

APPENDIX B

Weapons Used by UK Police Forces (2025)

Police forces throughout the UK use several different firearms. The most popular ones are listed below.

Pistols

- **Glock – 17**. This 9-mm pistol is the most-used police handgun throughout the UK.
- **Sig Sauer P250**. This 9-mm pistol is used by both the Cleveland and Essex police forces.
- **Walther P99**. This weapon is used by Nottinghamshire Police Authorised Firearms Officers (AFOs).
- **Sig-Sauer P226**. This 9-mm pistol is used by both Northamptonshire and Kent police forces.
- **Smith & Wesson M&P40**. This pistol is used by the Greater Manchester Police Tactical Firearms Unit.
- **Sig Pro 250**. This 9-mm pistol is used by Essex Police.

Carbines

- **Heckler & Koch MP5SF**. This is a 9-mm carbine, the single-fire version.

- **Heckler & Koch G36C**. This is a 5.56-mm semi-automatic carbine. The G36C-SF and the MP5SF are the most-carried police armed response unit carbines throughout the UK.
- **Heckler & Koch G36K**. This is a more powerful version of the G36C and is used by the North Yorkshire Police Firearms Support Unit (FSU).
- **Sig 552 Commando**. This is a short-barrelled 5.56-mm carbine and is the weapon of choice of Derbyshire Constabulary.
- **LMT Defender AR-15**. Used by AFOs in the Cheshire/North Wales policing area. It is also used by British Transport Police (BTP) officers when carrying out patrols of railway stations, as well as by their armed response units.
- **Heckler & Koch HK53**. Is a 5.56-mm semi-automatic carbine used by both Cumbria and Glasgow police forces.
- **Heckler & Koch HK416C**. The Hampshire Constabulary and the Thames Valley Police Tactical Firearms Department use this particular weapon.
- **Sig SG516**. This 5.56-mm carbine is used by the Metropolitan Police's SCO19 Tactical Support Teams, as well as their CTSFOs.

Sniper / Marksman Rifles

- **Tikka T3 Rifle Bolt Action Rifle**. This weapon is used by Essex and Northumbria police forces.
- **Heckler & Koch 417**. A semi-automatic 7.62-mm x 51-mm rifle used by Essex Police.
- **Blaser 93**. This is a German-made bolt-action rifle used by Avon & Somerset Constabulary.

Shotguns

- **Remington 870**. A 12-gauge pump action shotgun.
- **Benelli M1**. A semi-automatic 12-gauge shotgun.
- **Benelli Nova/Super Nova**. This is used by Essex Police.

Less-than-Lethal Weapons

- **Heckler & Koch L104A12 37mm launcher.** A 'riot gun' that fires an Attenuating Energy Projectile (AEP), otherwise known as a 'plastic bullet'. The weapon is fitted with a L18A1/2 sight.
- **X25 TASER.** Fires high-voltage wires attached to darts in order to incapacitate the suspect and is used by most UK police forces.

Sources

The Thin Green Line: The History of the Royal Ulster Constabulary by Richard Doherty (2005)
Report on the Hungerford shootings by Mr Colin Smith, CVO, QPM
The Birmingham Journal
The Police Guardian
The Scotsman
Lancashire Police Museum
Cheshire Police Museum
Cambridgeshire Police History
West Midlands Police
Leicestershire Police Historical Archive
Gwent Police
North Yorkshire Police
The Glasgow Police Museum
Gloucestershire Constabulary
Police Constable Aidrian Smart – Essex Police (Retired)
Police Constable Chris Clarke – Cheshire Police (Retired)
Police Constable Anthony Long – Metropolitan Police (Retired)

Index 215

Rodney, Azelle, 162, 163, 164, 165, 166, 167, 168
Royal Irish Constabulary (RIC), 50, 51
Royal Ulster Constabulary, 51, 52
Ruger, .223 Rifle, 87
Ryan, Michael Robert, 138, 139, 140, 141, 142, 143, 144, 145, 146, 147

SCO19 (Specialist Command 19), 8
SO14 (Specialist Operations 14), 10
Shorthouse, John, 72, 73
Shoulders, Sergeant Basil, 58
Sidney Street Siege, 6
Sig Pro Self-Loading Pistol, 40
Sig P50 Self-Loading Pistol, 40
Sim, John, 104, 105, 106
Smart, Constable Aidrian, 80, 81, 82, 84, 85, 86, 87, 88, 89, 90, 92
Smith & Wesson, 57, 72, 82, 87
SAS (Special Air Service), 63, 155, 200
Special Branch, 90
Special Escort Group, 10

SFO (Specialist Firearms Officer), 39, 40
SOU (Special Operations Unit), 77
Statute of Winchester, 2
Sudanese Airlines Hijacking, 150, 151, 152, 153, 154, 155, 156, 157

TASER, 40, 48
TFC (Tactical Firearms Commander), 84
TFG (Tactical Firearms Group), 19, 21, 26, 40, 44, 45, 46, 47, 83, 88
Tikka T3 Volt Action Rifle, 40
TPU (Trojan Proactive Unit), 9
TST (Tactical Support Team), 9

Ulster Special Constabulary, 50

Waldorf, Stephen, 116, 118, 119
West Mercia Constabulary, 69
West Midlands Police, 64, 70, 71, 76
Whitelaw, William (Home Secretary), 120
Wilson, Howard, 103, 105, 106
Witney, John Edward, 98, 99, 100

Donaldson, Ian, 104, 105, 106
Duddy, John, 98, 99, 100

Fairweather, Mervyn, 124, 126, 129, 132
Fielding, Henry, 2, 3
Fielding, John, 2, 3
FOU (Firearms Operations Unit), 71, 74, 75
FSU (Force Support Unit), 22, 43, 44, 45, 46, 47, 48, 53, 54, 55, 57, 82, 83, 123, 125, 126, 152, 153, 157

G36C, Heckler & Koch, 40, 163
George Medal, 67, 75
Glock 17, 40, 56
Gosford Street, 67
Grainger, Anthony, 185, 186, 187, 188
Groce, Dorothy 'Cherry', 134, 135, 136, 137

Harvey, Graham, 114
Howe, Paul, 107, 108, 112, 113, 114, 115

Jeffs, Charles, 67
Jocelyn, Ralph John, 4

Kabba, Chris, 201, 202, 203, 204

L1004A2 Launcher, Heckler & Koch, 40
Lambourne Road Siege, 60, 62

Leicestershire Police, 60
Long, Anthony, 168, 169, 170

Manners, Constable John, 111
Markham QPM, Chief Inspector Geoffrey, 41
Martin, David, 116, 117, 118, 119
Masood, Khalid, 195, 196, 197
Ministry of Defence Police, 1
Moat, Raoul, 179, 180, 181, 182, 183, 184
MO19 (Metropolitan Operations 19), 8
MP5, Heckler & Koch, 25, 26, 27, 40, 87, 156
MSG99 Rifle, Heckler & Kock, 56

National Police Firearms Training Curriculum (NPFTC), 18
Netherby Hall, 66
Nikoloff, Sabi, 60, 61, 62

PADP (Parliamentary and Diplomatic Protection), 10
Palmer, Constable Keith, 195, 196, 197
Peel, Sir Robert, 1, 31
Police Service of Northern Ireland, 50, 51, 52

Rathband, Constable David, 182
Rhymes, John, 125
Richards, Colin, 127, 128, 129, 130, 131
Roberts, Harry Maurice, 98, 99, 100

Index

417 Semi-Automatic Rifle, Heckler & Koch, 40

ABC Squad (Armed Besieged Criminal Squad), 57, 58
AET (Armed Emergency Team), 57, 58
AFO (Authorised Firearms Officer), 8, 11, 12, 16, 18, 19, 21, 37, 38, 39, 45, 53, 54, 55, 69, 70, 82
Annesley, Sir Hugh, 51
ARV (Armed Response Vehicle), 8, 39, 121
Ashley, James, 158, 159, 160, 161
ASP (Armament Systems and Procedures), 7
Audux in Periculis, 75
Auxiliaries, The, 50

Baker, Jermaine, 189, 190, 191, 192, 193
Benelli Nova Pump Action Shotgun, 40
Beretta, 40, 87
Bishop, Brian 'Bill', 122, 123, 124, 125, 126, 128, 129, 130, 131, 132, 133

Black and Tans, 50
Blake, Sergeant Martyn, 203, 204
Borough Market, 198, 199, 200
Bow Street Runners, 3
Bowers, Gus, 58, 59
Branham, Mick, 58
Braybrook Street, 97, 98
British Transport Police, 1

Carlton, Constable Gavin, 74
CFU (Central Firearms Unit), 57, 58
Cheshire Constabulary, 53, 55, 56
Churchill, Winston, 6
CID, 43, 44
Civil Nuclear Constabulary, 1
College of Policing, 11
CTSFO (Counter Terrorist Specialist Firearms Officer), 9, 39, 40

Dawkes, Constable Clive, 62, 63
Dear, Chief Constable Geoffrey, 73, 76
De Menezes, Jean Charles, 171, 172, 173, 174, 175, 176, 177, 178
Desert Storm, Operation, 28, 29

Stephen has co-written three crime thrillers, with another writing partner, Chris Burch, which were published between 2010 and 2012, and centre round a fictional detective named Terry Danvers.

Other works he has had published by Pen & Sword include:

The Surrender of Singapore: Three Years of Hell 1942-45 (2017)
Against All Odds: Walter Tull, The Black Lieutenant (2018)
Animals in the Great War (2018) (co-written with Tanya Wynn)
A History of the Royal Hospital Chelsea – 1682-2017: The Warriors Repose. (co-written with Tanya Wynn) (2019)
Disaster before D-Day: Unravelling the Tragedy of Slapton Sands (2019)
Mystery of Missing Flight F-BELV (2020)
City of London at War: 1938 - 45 (2020)
Holocaust: The Nazis' Wartime Jewish Atrocities (2020)
Churchill's Flawed Decisions: Errors in Office of the Greatest Britain (2020)
The Lancastria Tragedy: Sinking and Cover-up 1940 (2020)
The Rise & Fall of Imperial Japan (2020)
The Shetland 'Bus': Transporting Secret Agents Across The North Sea (2021)
Dunkirk and the Aftermath (2021)
St Nazaire Raid, 1942 (2022)
The Blackout Ripper: A Serial Killer in London, 1942 (2022)
HMS Turbulent (2023)
Dieppe, 1942 (2023)
Battle of Itter Castle, 1945 (2024)
Operation North Pole (2024)
Escaping Stalag Luft III (2025)

Author Biography

Stephen is a very happily retired Police officer having served with Essex Police as a Constable for thirty years between 1983 and 2013. He is married to Tanya who is also his best friend.

Both his sons, Luke and Ross, were members of the armed forces, collectively serving five tours of Afghanistan between 2008 and 2013. Both were injured on their first tour. This led to his first book; **'Two Sons in a Warzone – Afghanistan: The True Story of a Fathers Conflict'**, which was published in October 2010.

Both of his grandfathers served in and survived the First World War, one with the Royal Irish Rifles, the other in the Mercantile Navy, whilst his father was a member of the Royal Army Ordinance Corp during and after the Second World War.

When he is not writing, Stephen and Tanya enjoy the simplicity of going out for a morning coffee or walking their four German Shepherd dogs early each morning, whilst most sensible people are still fast asleep in their beds.

Stephen corroborated with one of his writing partners, Ken Porter on a previous book published in August 2012, **'German POW Camp 266 – Langdon Hills.'** It spent six weeks as the number one best-selling book in Waterstones, Basildon between March and April 2013. They have also collaborated on four books in the Towns & Cities in the Great War series by Pen and Sword. Stephen has also written other titles for the same series of books.